Windows® Me
Made Simple

P.K. McBride

**MADE SIMPLE
BOOKS**

OXFORD • AUCKLAND • BOSTON • JOHANNESBURG • MELBOURNE • NEW DELHI

Made Simple
An imprint of Butterworth-Heinemann
Linacre House, Jordan Hill, Oxford OX2 8DP
225 Wildwood Avenue, Woburn MA 01801-2041
A division of Reed Educational and Professional Publishing Ltd

ℛ   A member of the Reed Elsevier plc group

First published 2000
© P.K. McBride 2000

TRADEMARKS/REGISTERED TRADEMARKS
Computer hardware and software brand names mentioned in this book are protected
by their respective trademarks and are acknowledged.

British Library Cataloguing in Publication Data
A catalogue record for this book is available from the British Library

ISBN 0 7506 5237 3

⚘ Typeset by Elle and P.K. McBride, Southampton

Icons designed by Sarah Ward © 1994
Printed and bound in Great Britain

FOR EVERY TITLE THAT WE PUBLISH, BUTTERWORTH-HEINEMANN
WILL PAY FOR BTCV TO PLANT AND CARE FOR A TREE.

Contents

Preface

Windows, in its various forms, is now established as the world's leading operating system for personal computers. Windows Me is the latest version, and one designed with home and small office users in mind.

Windows Me Made Simple has been written mainly for the new computer user. The book starts by looking at the basic concepts and techniques of working with Windows – making choices, using the Help system and managing the screen.

Chapters 4 and 5 will show you how to organise your disks, so that you can store files safely and efficiently – and find them when you want them. We return to disks in Chapter 9, where we'll look at how to keep them in good working order.

One of the attractive features of Windows is that it lets you customise your system to suit the way that you work. In Chapters 6 and 7 you will see how to do this. Another of its attractive features is the ease with which it can be connected to peripherals and other PCs. You will see this in Chapters 8 and 10, *Printers* and *Home networking*.

In Chapter 11, we will have a quick look at a few of the accessories, then in the final chapter we will step away from the desktop into the wider world of the Internet. There is no space in this small book to do justice to this vast topic, but I hope that you will at least get a sense of its possibilities – then turn to *The Internet Made Simple* to find out more!

I have aimed to give you enough to be able to start using Windows quickly and confidently. Once you have got into the Window's way of doing things, you will find it easy to extend your skills and knowledge.

P.K. McBride, 2000

Take note

PCs running Windows 98 PCs can be upgraded to Windows Me – providing that they have sufficient RAM (minimum 32Mb) and hard disk space (minimum 1Gb, but realistically at least 2Gb).

1 Start here

The Desktop

Windows is a Graphical User Interface (or GUI, pronounced *gooey*). What this means is that you work mainly by using the mouse to point at and click on symbols on the screen, rather than by typing commands. It is largely intuitive – i.e. the obvious thing to do is probably the right thing – and it is tolerant of mistakes. Many can be corrected as long as you tackle them straight away, and many others can be corrected easily, even after time has passed.

One of the key ideas behind the design of Windows is that you should treat the screen as you would a desk, which is why Windows refers to the screen as the *desktop*. This is where you lay out your papers, books and tools, and you can arrange them to suit your own way of working. You may want to have more than one set of papers on the desktop at a time – so Windows lets you run several programs at once. You may want to have all your papers visible, for comparing or transferring data; you may want to concentrate on one, but have the others to hand. These – and other arrangements – are all possible.

Each program runs in its own window, and these can be arranged side by side, overlapping, or with the one you are working on filling the desktop and the others tucked out of the way, but still instantly accessible.

Just as there are many ways of arranging your desktop, so there are many ways of working with it – in fact, you are sometimes spoiled for choice!

It's your desktop. How you arrange it, and how you use it is up to you. This book will show you the simplest ways to use Windows Me effectively.

❑ What you see on screen when you start Windows depends upon your Desktop settings and the shortcuts – the icons that you can click on to start progams – you are using.

❑ What the screen looks like once you are into your working session, is infinitely variable.

❑ Certain principles always apply and certain things are always there. It is the fact that all Windows applications share a common approach that makes Windows so easy to use.

Shortcuts – instant access to programs.
You can create shortcuts (page 74).

Desktop – you can change the background
picture or pattern and its colours (page 95).

Menu bar – gives access to
a program's commands.

Program windows – adjust their
size and placing to suit yourself.

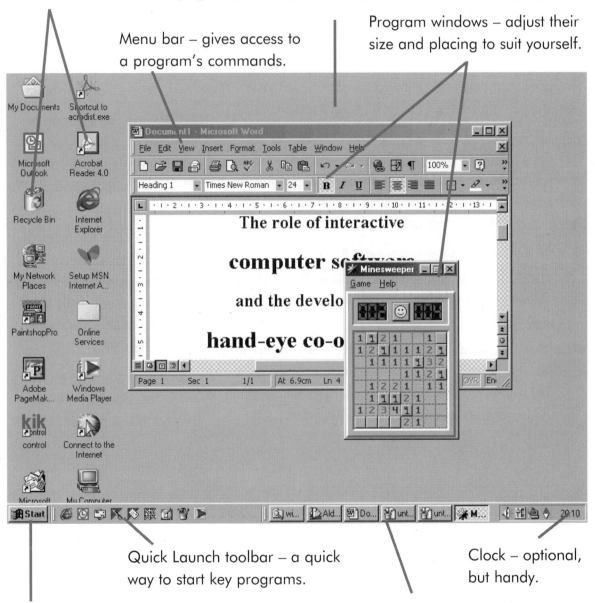

Quick Launch toolbar – a quick
way to start key programs.

Clock – optional,
but handy.

Start button – you should be
able to start any program on
your PC from its menu.

Taskbar – when a program is running,
it has a button here. Click on a button
to bring its program to the top.

Taming the mouse

You can't do much in Windows until you have tamed the mouse. It is used for locating the cursor, for selecting from menus, highlighting, moving and changing the size of objects, and much more. It won't bite, but it will wriggle until you have shown it who's in charge.

To control the mouse effectively you need a mouse mat or a thin pad of paper – mice don't run well on hard surfaces.

The mouse and the cursor

Moving the mouse rolls the ball inside it. The ball turns the sensor rollers and these transmit the movement to the cursor. Straightforward? Yes, but note these points.

- If you are so close to the edge of the mat that you cannot move the cursor any further, pick up the mouse and plonk it back into the middle. If the ball doesn't move, the cursor doesn't move.

- You can set up the mouse so that when the mouse is moved faster, the cursor moves further. (See *Adjusting the mouse*, page 98.) Watch out for this when working on other people's machines.

Tip

A clean mouse is a happy mouse. If it starts to play up, take out the ball and clean it and the rollers with a damp tissue. Check for fluff build-up on the roller axles and remove any present with tweezers.

Mouse actions

Point – move the cursor with your fingers off the buttons.

Click the left button to select a file, menu item or other object.

Click the right button to open a menu of commands that apply to the object beneath the pointer.

Double-click to run programs. You can set the gap between clicks to suit yourself. (See *Adjusting the mouse*, page 98.)

Drag – keep the left button down while moving the mouse. Used for resizing, drawing and similar jobs.

Drag and drop – drag an object and release the left button when it is in the right place. Used for moving objects.

Key guide

[Esc] – to Escape from trouble. Use it to cancel bad choices.

[Tab] – move between objects on screen.

[Caps Lock] – only put this on when you want to type a lot of capitals. The Caps Lock light shows if it is on.

[Shift] – use it for capitals and the symbols on the number keys.

[Ctrl] or [Control] – used with other keys to give keystroke alternatives to mouse commands.

⊞ – same as clicking ⊞Start on the screen.

[Alt] – used, like [Ctrl], with other keys.

[Backspace] – rubs out the character to the left of the text cursor.

[Enter] – used at the end of a piece of text or to start an operation.

[Delete] – deletes files, folders and screen objects. Use with care.

The keyboard

Most Windows Me operations can be handled quite happily by the mouse alone, leaving the keyboard for data entry. However, keys are necessary for some jobs, and if you prefer typing to mousing, it is possible to do most jobs from the keyboard. The relevant ones are shown here.

The function keys

Some operations can be run from these – for instance, **[F1]** starts up the Help system in any Windows application.

The control sets

The **Arrow** keys can often be used instead of the mouse for moving the cursor. Above them are more movement keys, which will let you jump around in text. **[Insert]** and **[Delete]** are also here.

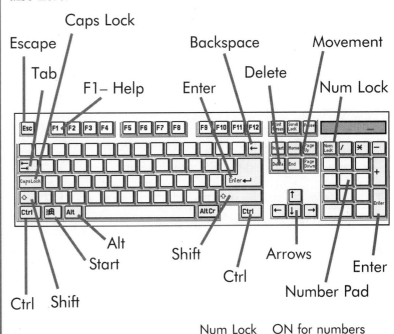

Num Lock ON for numbers
OFF for movement

5

Making choices

There are many situations where you have to specify a filename or an option. Sometimes you have to type in what you want, but in most cases, it only takes a click of the mouse or a couple of keystrokes.

Menus

To pull one down from the menu bar click on it, or press **[Alt]** (the key marked '**Alt**') and the underlined letter – usually the initial.

To select an item from a menu, click on it or type its underlined letter.

Some items are *toggles*. Selecting them turns an option on or off. ✔ beside the name shows that the option is on.

▶ after an item shows that another menu leads from it.

If you select an item with three dots ... after it, a dialog box will open to get more information from you.

Click or press [Alt] + [V]

Point to open
Sub-menu

Toggle

Dialog box
will follow

Click to get to its panel

Dialog boxes

These vary, but will usually have:

- OK to click when you have set the options, selected the file or whatever;

- Apply fix the options selected so far, but do not leave the box;

- Cancel in case you decide the whole thing was a mistake;

- Help or ? to get Help on items in the box.

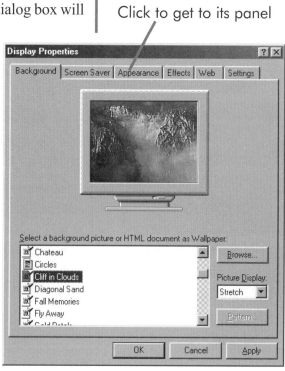

Tabs and panels

Some dialog boxes have several sets of options in them, each on a separate panel. These are identified by tabs at the top. Click on a tab to bring its panel to the front. Usually clicking **OK** on any panel will close the whole box. Use **Apply** when you have finished with one panel but want to explore others before closing.

Check boxes

These are used where there are several options, and you can use as many as you like at the same time.

✔ in the box shows that the option has been selected.

If the box is grey and the caption faint, the option is 'greyed out' – not available at that time for the selected item.

Take note

Most menus drop down from the top bar. The Start menu (page 9) is different – it pops up.

Only this one

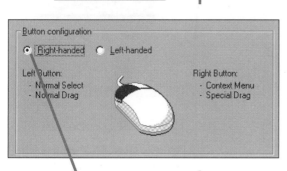

Radio buttons

These are used for either/or options. Only one of the set can be selected.

The selected option is shown by black blob in the middle.

This one please

Drop-down lists

If a slot has a down arrow button on its right, click the button to drop down a list.

Click on an item in the list to select.

Click here...

... to select from the list

Take note

Some commands have keyboard shortcuts – often [Ctrl] + a letter. Look out for these on the menus.

Context menus

If you click the right button on almost any object on screen in Windows Me, a short menu will open beside it. This contains a set of commands and options that can be applied to the object.

What is on the menu depends upon the type of object and its *context* – hence the name. Two are shown here to give an idea of the possibilities.

Properties

Most menus have a **Properties** item. The contents of its dialog box also vary according to the nature of the object. For shortcuts, like the one for the Phone Dialer shown below, there is a *Shortcut* panel that controls the link to the program. The (hidden) *General* panel has a description of the file – this panel is in every file's Properties box.

Files can be opened, sent to a removable disk or off in the mail, and deleted – amongst other things.

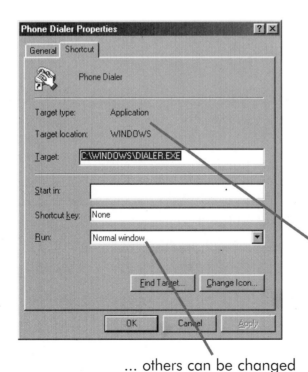

The Clock can be adjusted, and as it is on the Taskbar, you can also arrange the screen display from this menu.

Some properties are there for information only ...

... others can be changed

The Start menu

Clicking on  **Start** at the bottom left of the screen, takes you into the menu system from which you can run applications, get Help, search for files and other things, customize your system and close down at the end of a session.

The Start menu has eight or nine options:

Windows Update will take you online to Microsoft's site to download any new versions of the Windows files.

Programs is the main route to your applications. Leading from this is a second level of program folders, and selecting from there takes you to the icons for the programs in each folder.

Documents holds a list of recently-used document files. Selecting one from this list will run the relevant application and open the file for you to work on (see page 10).

Settings is used to customize the Desktop and other aspects of the system (Chapter 7), set up printers (Chapter 8) and even rewrite the Start menu (Chapter 6).

Search will track down files and folders on your computer, on your network and on the Internet, and also help you to find people on the Internet.

Help is one way into the Help system (Chapter 2).

Run lets you run a named application or starts up work on a document. This is mainly used for running DOS programs.

Log off... will be present if the PC is on a network. It allows the current user to stop using the PC – and for someone else to start – without turning it off.

Shut down is the only safe way to end a session.

Take note

Windows uses the word DOCUMENT to refer to any file that is created by an application. A word- processed report is obviously a document, but so is a picture file from a graphics package, data files from spreadsheets, video clips, sound files – in fact any file produced by any program.

Running a program

The programs already on your PC, and virtually all of those that you install later, will have an entry in the **Programs** menu. Selecting one from here will run the program, ready for you to start work.

A program can also be run by selecting a document that was created by it. Those documents used most recently are stored in the **Documents** menu.

Basic steps

❑ Running a program

1 Click [Start].

2 Point to Programs.

3 Point to the menu that contains the program – you may have to point to the next menu level.

4 Click on the name to run the program.

❑ From Documents

5 Click [Start].

6 Point to Documents

7 Click on the file to get started on it.

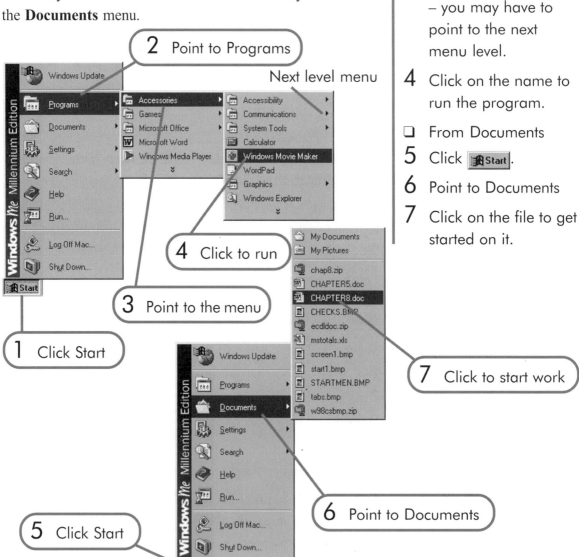

Basic steps

1 Click **Start** and point to Programs.

2 Pick a recently-used program from the reduced display.

Or

3 Click [ⅹ   ] on any menu.

4 Pick from the full set.

The Start menu is a smart menu – it notices which programs you use and adjusts the display to suit. After a few days' you will see that the Start menu no longer displays those programs and submenus that you have not used. They are still there, but tucked away out of sight. When needed, the menu can be opened fully so that all the options are visible, and once you have used a program or made a selection from a submenu, it will be included in the Start menu display again.

To open up the menus, click the double arrow at the bottom of any one of them. Once you have opened any menu, all of them will be displayed in full.

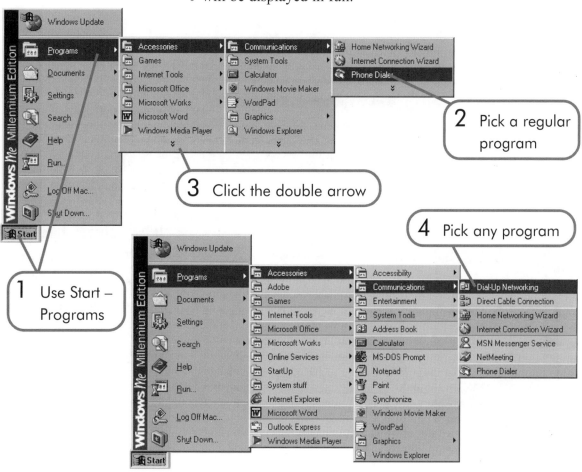

2 Pick a regular program

3 Click the double arrow

4 Pick any program

1 Use Start – Programs

Shutting down

When you have finished work on your computer, you must shut it down properly, and not just turn it off. This is essential. During a working session, application programs and Windows Me itself may have created temporary files – and any data files that you have been editing may still be open in memory and not yet written safely to disk. A proper shut down closes and stores open files and removes unwanted ones.

Restart

The Shut Down dialog box offers a Restart option. You may need this after installing new software or hardware. It is also one way to solve problems – see opposite for more on this.

see opposite for more on this.

Basic steps

Basic steps

1 Click Start.

2 Select Shut Down.

3 Check the option – it will be on whatever you last used, Shut down or Restart – and change it if necessary.

4 Click OK.

Shut Down Windows

What do you want the computer to do?

Restart

Shut down
Restart
Windows again.

OK   Cancel   Help

3 Restart?

4 Click OK

Windows Update

Programs

Documents

Settings

Search

Help

Run...

Log Off Mac...

Shut Down...

Windows Me Millennium Edition

Start

2 Choose Shut Down

1 Click Start

If you start a shut down by mistake – easily done! – you can stop it

Take note

If you simply turn off the PC, or have to use the Restart button, when it starts up again, Windows will offer to check your hard drive(s) in case there is a problem. The check only takes a few moments and is normally worth doing.

Coping with crashes

❏ Misbehaving program

1 Open the program's File menu and select Exit (or Close) – saving files if prompted.

2 Restart the program.

❏ Hung system

3 Press [Ctrl] + [Alt] + [Delete] together.

4 At the Close Program dialog box, select the one marked 'not responding' and click End Task .

5 Restart the program.

❏ Dead keyboard

6 Press the Restart button on front of the PC.

Windows Me is a pretty stable system and most commercial software is very thoroughly tested, but sometimes things go wrong. A 'crash' can can be at several levels.

● A program may simply misbehave – it will still run, but not respond or update the screen correctly. Close it – saving any open files – and run it again. If it still behaves badly, close down all your programs and restart the PC.

● The system will 'hang' – i.e. nothing is happening and it will not respond to the mouse or normal keyboard commands. If the **[Ctrl] + [Alt] + [Del]** keystroke works, you can close the offending application, which may get things moving again.

● You get a total lock up where it will not pick up **[Ctrl] + [Alt] + [Del]**. Press the little restart button on the front of the PC. It is there for just these times!

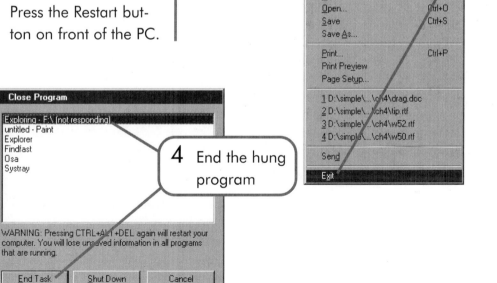

1 Use File – Exit

4 End the hung program

Summary

- ❑ Windows is an intuitive system – if something *feels* right, it probably *is* right.

- ❑ All Windows software works in much the same way, so once you have got the hang of one program, you are half way to learning the next.

- ❑ The mouse is an important tool. Practise using it – a good excuse for playing the games!

- ❑ Some operations are easier with keys, and just a few can only be done from the keyboard.

- ❑ Selections can usually be made by picking from a list or clicking on a button or check box.

- ❑ Every object has a context menu containing those commands that you may want to use with it.

- ❑ The Start button is the main way into the system. Get to know your way around its menus.

- ❑ Applications can be run directly from the Programs menu, or through files in the Documents list.

- ❑ The Start menu is smart. It normally only displays the programs you have used recently. The full menus can be opened if wanted.

- ❑ You must Shut Down properly at the end of a work session.

- ❑ You may have to restart the system after installing new kit or to recover from a program crash.

2 Help!

Help with applications

All modern Windows applications – i.e. anything written for Windows 98 or Me – has the same style of Help system. Older Windows programs had a slightly different Help system.

You can get Help in several ways:

● Use the Help menu on applications and accessories;

● Click ? for 'query' Help on dialog boxes.

● Press **[F1]** – anywhere, any time – to get into the Help system.

In all application Help systems there are three approaches:

● an organised **Contents** list;

● **Index**ed Help pages;

● a word-based **Search** facility.

Basic steps

1 Click on Help on the menu bar and ....

2 ... select Help Topics.

Or

3 ... select Contents and Index.

Or

4 Press [F1].

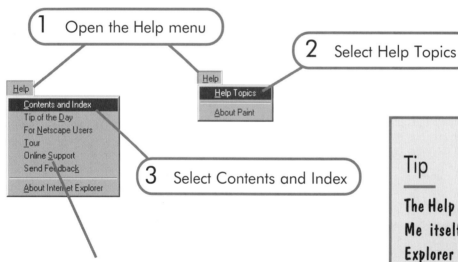

1 Open the Help menu

2 Select Help Topics

Help
Contents and Index
Tip of the Day
For Netscape Users
Tour
Online Support
Send Feedback
About Internet Explorer

Help
Help Topics
About Paint

3 Select Contents and Index

Most applications today also offer additional support through the Internet

Tip

The Help system in Windows Me itself and in Windows Explorer is slightly different from that in applications – see pages **22 to 25.**

Basic steps

1 Click the Contents tab if this panel is not at the front already.

2 Click on a ![book icon] icon or its text to see the page titles – or the next level of books.

3 Click on a ![page icon] icon or its text to read a page.

4 Click on <u>Related Topics</u> to reach any linked pages

5 Click ![X] to exit Help.

The Toolbar

![Hide icon] Closes the Tabs (the left of the window) and is replaced by ![Show icon] to reopen it.

![Back icon] Return to previous Help page.

![Forward icon] On to next (visited) Help page.

![Options icon] For keyboard control – can be opened by [Alt]–[O].

![Web Help icon] Link to Microsoft Web site.

Contents

This approach treats the Help pages as a book. You scan through the headings to find a section that seems to cover what you want, and open that to see the page titles. (Some sections have sub-sections, making it a two or three-stage process to get to page titles.)

Some Help pages have <u>Related topics</u> links to take you on to further pages.

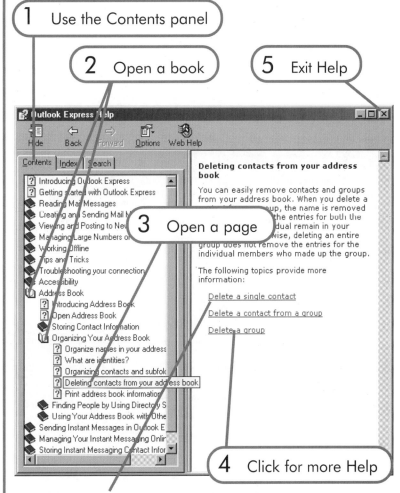

1 Use the Contents panel

2 Open a book

5 Exit Help

3 Open a page

4 Click for more Help

<u>Underlined words</u> link to another Help page or to a definition of a term.

Using the Index

Though the Contents are good for getting an overview of how things work, if you want help on a specific problem – usually the case – you are better off with the Index.

This is organised through an cross-referenced list of terms. The main list is alphabetical, with sub-entries, just like the index in a book. And, as with an index in a book, you can plough through it slowly from the top, or skip through to find the words that start with the right letters. Once you find a suitable entry, you can display the list of cross-referenced topics and pick one of those.

Basic steps

1   Click the Index tab.
2   Start to type a word into the slot then scroll to the topic.
3   Select an Index entry.
4   Click Display .
5   Pick a topic from the Topics Found list.
6   Click Display .
❑   If there is only one relevant topic page, the system will take you directly to it after Step 4.

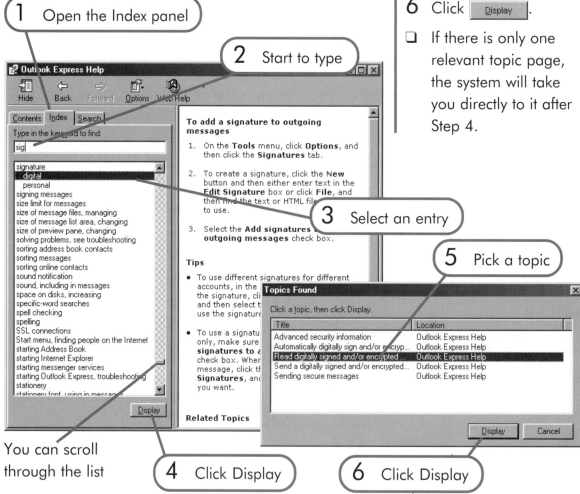

1 Open the Index panel

2 Start to type

3 Select an entry

5 Pick a topic

You can scroll through the list

4 Click Display

6 Click Display

18

Basic steps

1 Click the Search tab.
2 Type a keyword into the slot.
3 Click [List Topics].
4 Pick a topic from the list.
5 Click [Display].

Take note

A 'keyword' is simply a word which identifies what you are looking for.

Tip

Sometimes the screen is not redrawn properly after displaying the definition of an underlined term. Use Options – Refresh to restore the display.

Search for Help

On the Index panel you are hunting through the titles of Help pages. On the Search panel, the system looks for matching *keywords* within pages.

● A keyword can be any word which might occur in the pages that you are looking for.

● If you give two or more, the system will only list pages which contain all those words.

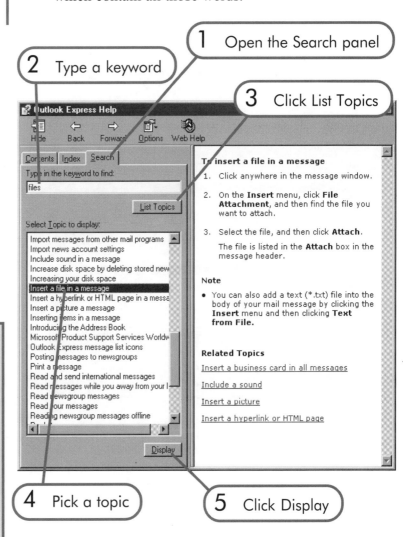

1 Open the Search panel

2 Type a keyword

3 Click List Topics

4 Pick a topic

5 Click Display

Finding Help

In older Windows applications you will meet this in place of the Search panel. It is based on the same principles – searching for matching words within Help pages – but is used in a slightly different way.

1 Open the Find panel.

2 Type your word into the top slot. As you type, words starting with the typed letters appear in the pane beneath.

3 If you want to narrow the search, go back to Step 2, type a space after your first word and give another.

4 Select the most suitable word from the Narrow the search pane.

5 Select a topic from the lower pane.

6 Click Display.

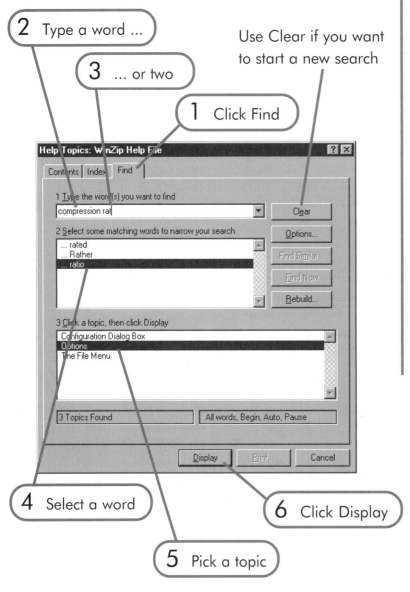

2 Type a word ...

3 ... or two

Use Clear if you want to start a new search

1 Click Find

4 Select a word

6 Click Display

5 Pick a topic

Take note

The first time you use Find for any application, a Wizard will run to create the word list. Take the Minimum option – it will do what you want.

Basic steps

1 On the Find panel, click [Options...].

2 Select All the words... where you are using several words to focus on one topic.

3 Select At least one... where you are giving alternatives, hoping that it recognises one.

4 Decide when you want the system to Begin searching.

5 Click [OK].

Find options

There are several Options that you can set to alter the nature of the search or narrow its scope.

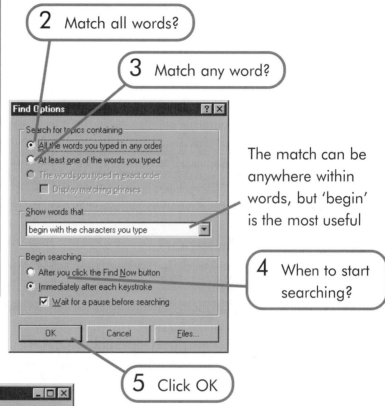

2 Match all words?

3 Match any word?

The match can be anywhere within words, but 'begin' is the most useful

4 When to start searching?

5 Click OK

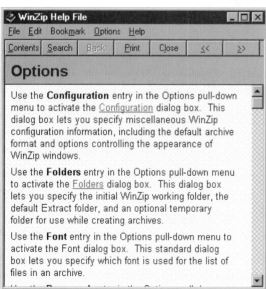

Older applications display Help pages in a separate window. With these, use Contents or Search to return to the main panel if you need more Help. The illustration comes from WinZip, a program that compresses and uncompresses files – an essential tool for anyone who intends to get material of the Internet. Find out more about it on the Web at http://www.winzip.com.

Help and support

Windows Me has its own special Help and Support system. It's very comprehensive and has some excellent features, but – most unhelpfully – it looks and feels different from the standard application Help systems. The same facilities are there, but with new names.

The Home section is the equivalent to Contents. Start to browse through the Help pages from here.

Basic steps

1 Click ▒Start▒ and select Help.

Or

2 In My Computer or Windows Explorer (see Chapter 4), use Help – Help Topics.

3 Click the underlined headings to browse through the contents.

2 Use Help – Help Topics

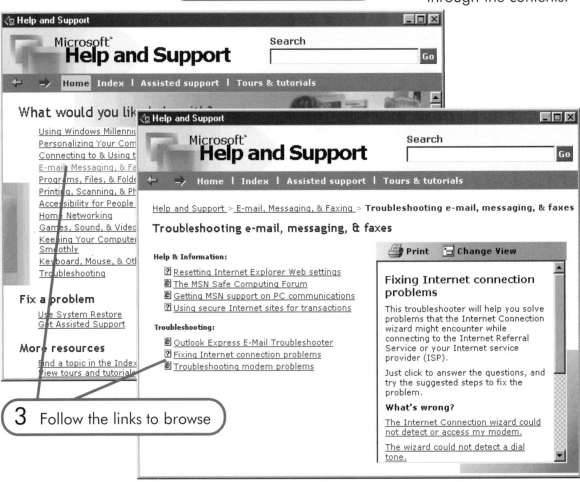

3 Follow the links to browse

Basic steps

1 Switch to the Index.

2 Start to type a word, then scroll to the topic.

3 Select an Index entry.

4 Click **Display** – you may be offered a choice of several relevant Help pages.

5 Click 🔳 to shrink the display – click 🔳 to restore the full view if needed later.

Help Index

This is almost identical to the Index part of the standard Help systems. Scroll through the index or enter the first few letters to jump to the right part of the list.

Change view

In any part of the Help system, once you have opened a Help page in the right-hand pane, you can use Change views to shrink the display so that only the Help page is visible.

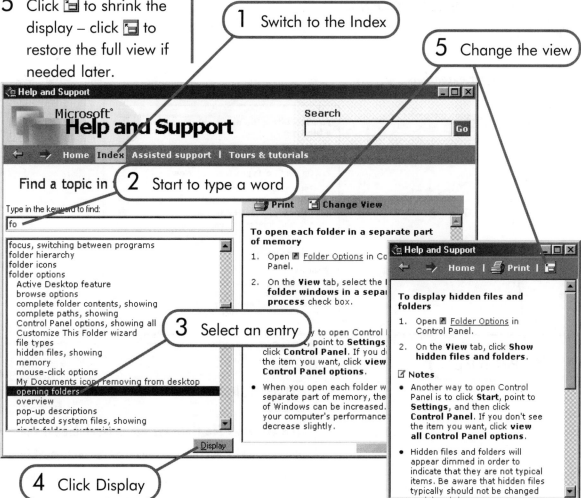

Searching for Help

You can run a search at any point in the Help system – the Search box is always there at the top of the Help and Support window.

● If you know what you are looking for, you can normally find it faster through a search than by using either the Home or Index sections.

Basic steps

1 Type a keyword into the Search box.

2 Click **Go**.

3 Pick a Help page from the list.

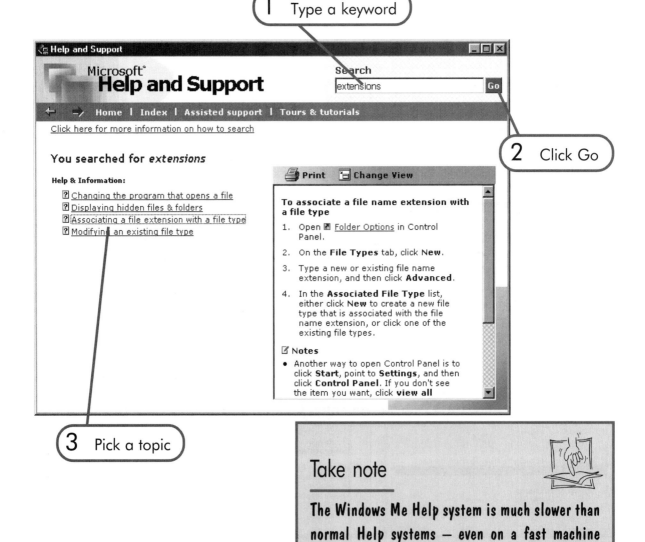

1 Type a keyword

2 Click Go

3 Pick a topic

Take note

The Windows Me Help system is much slower than normal Help systems — even on a fast machine there is a noticeable delay while it gets started.

Basic steps

1 Switch to Tours & tutorials.

2 Pick a topic.

3 Use the headings on the top on the left to navigate through the tour.

Tours & tutorials

Tours are simple, but useful introductions to new topics. Tutorials are interactive learning experiences – and there are very few of these. The Tours & tutorials section is the obvious place to start, but you will also find links to relevant tours or tutorials in many contents lists.

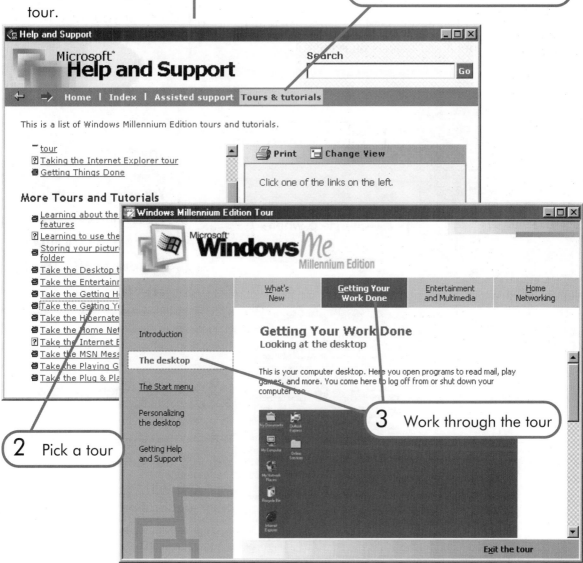

Instant Help

As well as the main Help system, Windows Me and Windows applications offer a couple of other useful forms of Help.

The query icon

All dialog boxes and panels in Windows Me and its components – and in any new or recent Windows applications – have an ⟨?⟩ icon on the top right of the status bar. You will also find an ⟨▶?⟩ icon on the toolbar of some applications. They can both be used for finding out more about objects on screen.

Basic steps

1 Click on the ⟨?⟩ or ⟨▶?⟩ icon.

2 Click the ⟨▶?⟩ cursor on the button, option or other item that you want to know about.

3 After you have read the Help box, click anywhere to close it.

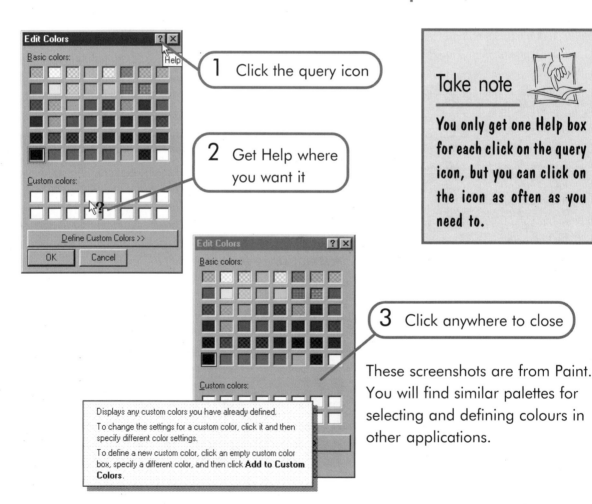

1 Click the query icon

2 Get Help where you want it

3 Click anywhere to close

Displays any custom colors you have already defined.

To change the settings for a custom color, click it and then specify different color settings.

To define a new custom color, click an empty custom color box, specify a different color, and then click **Add to Custom Colors**.

Take note

You only get one Help box for each click on the query icon, but you can click on the icon as often as you need to.

These screenshots are from Paint. You will find similar palettes for selecting and defining colours in other applications.

26

Help on icons

Tip

Even if the Help box doesn't give you enough information, it will give you the words you need to find more detailed Help. From the example on the right, we can get 'Fill', and using that in a Search gets us to detailed instructions on how to fill shapes with colour.

Icons are supposed to be self-explanatory, but their purpose cannot always be summed up in a small image. Never fear, help is near!

Let the cursor rest over an icon for a moment and a label will pop up to tell you what it is. If that isn't enough to tell you what it does, at least you have a name to look up in the Help Index.

Point and wait to see the icon's label

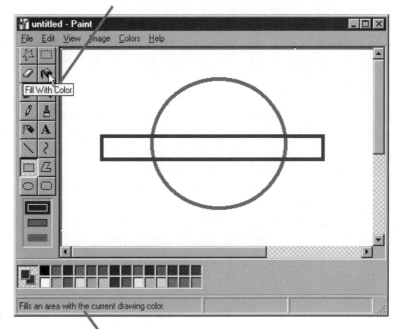

There's more help in the Status Bar

Take note

If a window is in Restore mode — i.e. smaller than the full screen (see page 32 for more) — the message area in the Status Bar may not be long enough to display the Help message in full.

Summary

- ❑ Help is always available.

- ❑ Use the Contents panel when you are browsing to see what topics are covered.

- ❑ Use the Index to go directly to the help on a specified operation or object.

- ❑ If you can't locate the Help in the Index, use the Search (Windows Me) or Find (older Windows applications) facility to track down the pages.

- ❑ Windows Me has a comprehensive – if a little slow – Help and Support system. This has its own special style and approach.

- ❑ The Tours & tutorials provide good introductions to some Windows Me topics.

- ❑ For Help with items in a dialog box or panel, click the query icon and point to the item.

- ❑ If you hold the cursor over an icon, a brief prompt will pop up to tell you what it does. There will also be a Help message in the Status Bar.

3 Window control

The window frame

This is more than just a pretty border. It contains all the controls you need for adjusting the display.

Frame edge

This has a control system built into it. When a window is in Restore mode – i.e. smaller than full-screen – you can drag on the edge to make it larger or smaller. (See *Changing the size*, page 37.)

Title bar

This is to remind you of where you are – the title bar of the active application (the one you are using) is blue; the bars of other open applications are grey. The bar is also used for moving the window. Drag on this and the window moves. (See *Moving windows*, page 36.)

Maximize, Minimize and Restore

These buttons change the display mode. Only one of Maximize and Restore will be visible at any one time. (See *Window modes*, page 32.)

Close

One of several ways to close a window and the program that was running in it. (See *Closing windows*, page 39.)

Control menu icon

There is no set image for this icon, as every application has its own, but clicking on whatever is here will open the Control menu. This can be used for changing the screen mode or closing the window. (See *Window modes*, page 32.) Double-clicking this icon will close down the window.

Take note

Most applications can handle several documents at once, each in its own window. These are used in almost the same way as program windows. The applications usually have a **Window** menu containing controls for the document windows.

30

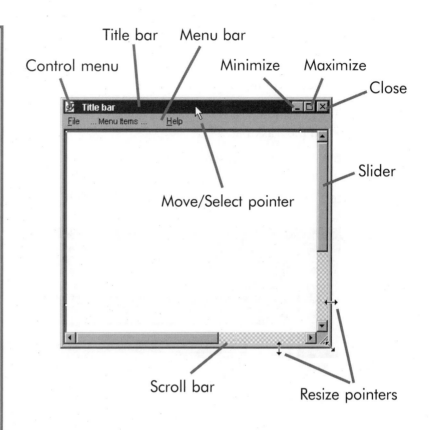

Menu bar

Immediately below the Title bar in an application's window is a bar containing the names of its menus. Clicking on one of these will drop down a list of commands.

Scroll bars

These are present on the right side and bottom of the frame if the display contained by the window is too big to fit within it. The **Sliders** in the Scroll bars show you where your view is, relative to the overall display. Moving these allows you to view a different part of the display. (See *Scrolling*, page 38.)

Window modes

All programs are displayed on screen in windows, and these can normally have three modes:

● Maximized – filling the whole screen;

● Minimized – not displayed, though still present as a button on the Task bar;

● Restore – adjustable in size and in position.

Take note

Some applications run in small, fixed size windows, so Maximize and Restore do not apply to them.

Maximized

In Restore mode

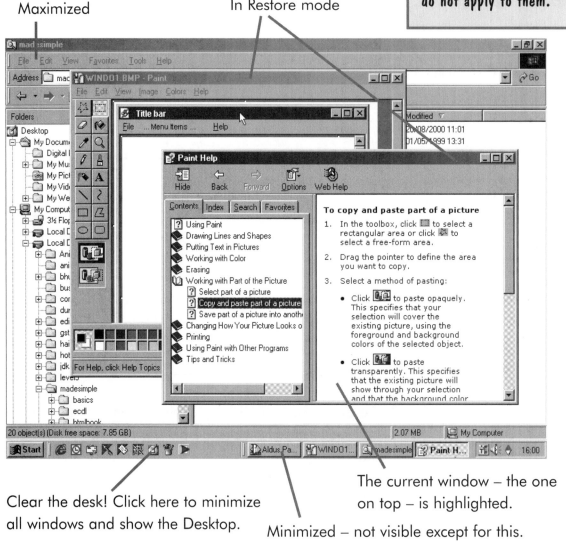

Clear the desk! Click here to minimize all windows and show the Desktop.

Minimized – not visible except for this.

The current window – the one on top – is highlighted.

Basic steps

- ❏ To make a window full-screen

  Click 🔲 or select Maximize from the Control Menu

- ❏ To restore a window to variable size

  Click 🔳 or select Restore from the Control Menu

- ❏ To shrink a window to an icon

  Click 🔳 or select Minimize from the Control Menu

Changing display modes

Clicking on the buttons in the top right corner of the frame is the simplest way to switch between **Maximize** and **Restore** modes, and to **Minimize** a window. If you prefer it can be done using the Control Menu.

The Control menu

Click the icon at the top left to open this. Options that they don't apply at the time will be 'greyed out'. The menu here came from a variable size window. One from a full-screen window would have **Move**, **Size** and **Maximize** in grey.

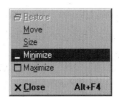

Using the Taskbar

Click a program's button to bring its window to the top.

Right-click the button to open the Control menu.

Left-click to activate

Right-click for the menu

Keyboard control

[Alt]–[Space] opens the Control menu of an application.

[Alt]–[-] (minus) opens the Control menu of a document.

Minimized documents

When you minimize a document window, within an application, it shrinks to a tiny title bar, with just enough room for a name and the icons. Click Maximize or Restore to open it out again.

Restore   Maximize

Arranging windows

If you want to have two or more windows visible at the same time, you will have to arrange them on your desktop. There are Windows tools that will do it for you, or you can do it yourself.

If you right-click the Taskbar, its menu has options to arrange the windows on the desktop. Open it and you will see **Cascade**, **Tile Vertical** and **Tile Horizontal**. Similar options are on the Window menu of most applications, though these only affect the layout *within* the programs.

Cascade places the windows overlapping with just the title bars of the back ones showing. You might just as well Maximize the current window, and use the Taskbar buttons to get to the rest.

Either of the Tile layouts can be the basis of a well-arranged desktop.

Basic steps

1 Maximize or Restore the windows that you want to include in the layout. Minimize those that you will not be using actively.

2 Right-click the Taskbar to open its menu.

3 Select Tile WIndows Horizontally or Tile Windows Vertically.

4 If you only want to work in one window at a time, Maximize it, and Restore it back into the arrangement when you have done.

Tip

If you want to adjust the balance of the layout, you can move and resize the windows.

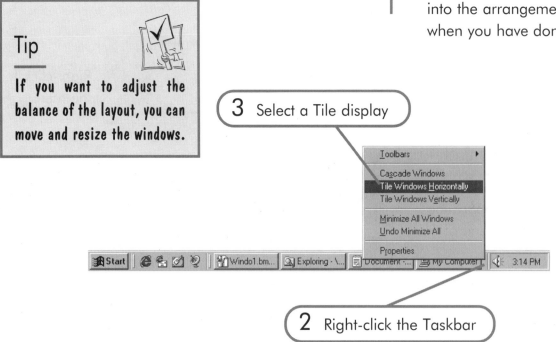

3 Select a Tile display

2 Right-click the Taskbar

Tile

Tip

Cascade displays work better than Tile displays on small screens.

Tile arranges open windows side by side (Vertical), or one above the other (Horizontal) – with more than three windows, the tiling is in both directions. As the window frames take up space, the actual working area is significantly reduced. Obviously, larger, high-resolution screens are better for multi-window work, but even on a 1024 x 768 display you cannot do much serious typing in a tiled window.

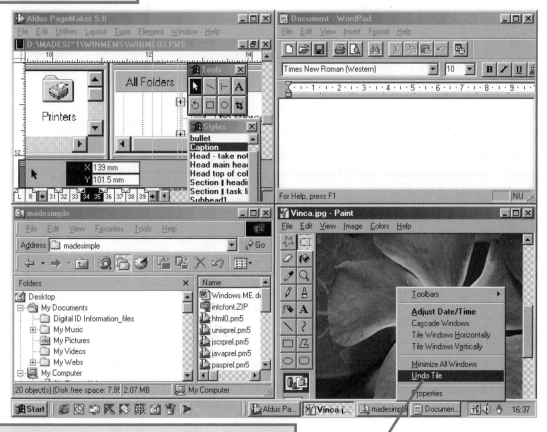

Tip

It is generally simplest to work with the active window Maximized and any others Minimized out of the way.

The Taskbar menu now has an Undo Tile option to restore your screen to its previous state.

Moving windows

When a window is in **Restore** mode – open but not full screen – it can be moved anywhere on the screen.

●   If you are not careful it can be moved almost off the screen! Fortunately, at least a bit of the title bar will still be visible, and that is the handle you need to grab to pull it back into view.

1 If the Title Bar isn't highlighted, click on the window to make it the active one.

2 Point at the Title Bar and hold the left button down.

3 Drag the window to its new position – you will only see a grey outline moving.

4 Release the button.

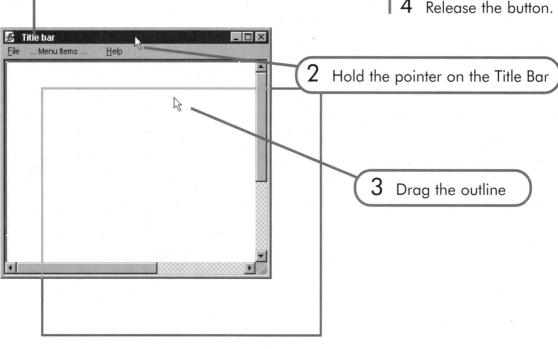

1 Make the window active

2 Hold the pointer on the Title Bar

3 Drag the outline

4 Release to drop into its new position

Basic steps

1 Move the pointer to the edge or corner that you want to pull in or out.

2 When you see the double-headed arrow, hold down the left mouse button and drag the outline to the required size.

3 Release the button.

When a window is in Restore mode, you can change its size and shape by dragging the edges of the frame to new positions.

Combined with the moving facility, this lets you arrange your desktop exactly the way you like it.

● The resize pointers only appear when the pointer is just on an edge, and they disappear again if you go too far. Practise! You'll soon get the knack of catching them.

You can drag any edge or corner

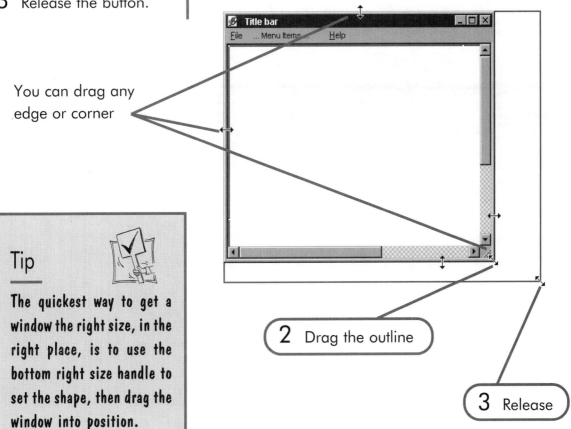

2 Drag the outline

3 Release

Tip

The quickest way to get a window the right size, in the right place, is to use the bottom right size handle to set the shape, then drag the window into position.

Scrolling

What you can see in a window is often only part of the story. The working area of the application may well be much larger. If there are scroll bars on the side and/or bottom of the window, this tells you that there is more material outside the frame. The scroll bars let you pull some of this material into view.

Tip

If a window is blank — and you think there should be something there — push the sliders to the very top and left. That's where your work is likely to be.

Basic scrolls

❑ Drag the slider ▮ to scroll the view in the window. Drag straight along the bar or it won't work!

❑ Click an arrow ▲ to edge the slider towards the arrow. Hold down for a slow continuous scroll.

❑ Click on the bar beside the Slider to make it jump towards the pointer.

Sliders

Arrow buttons

Working area

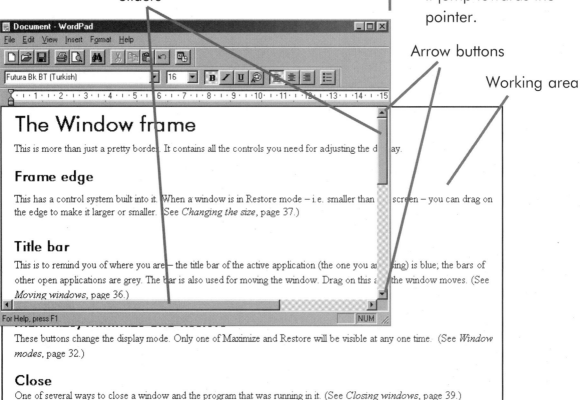

Closing windows

❑ Closing an active window

1 Click ⊠ or press [Alt]-[F4].

❑ Closing from the Taskbar

2 Right-click the progam's button to get its menu.

3 Select Close.

4 If you have forgotten to save your work, take the opportunity that is offered to you.

When you close a window, you close down the program that was running inside it.

If you haven't saved your work, most programs will point this out and give you a chance to save before closing.

There are at least five different ways of closing. Here are the simplest three:

● If the window is in Maximized or Restore mode, click the close icon at the top right of the Title bar. (If your mouse control is not too good, you may well do this when you are trying to Maximize the window!)

● If the window has been Minimized onto the Taskbar, right-click on its button to open the Control menu and use **Close**.

● If you prefer working from keys, press **[Alt]+[F4]**.

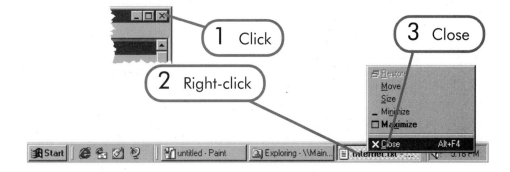

Tip
―――
When you have finished with a program, close it. Even Minimized windows use some memory and slow down performance.

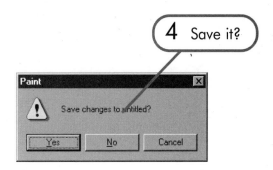

Summary

❏ You can move between windows by clicking on any visible part of them – though the active parts of the frame should be avoided.

❏ Windows can be displayed in Maximized (full-screen) or Restore (variable size) modes, or Mini-mized to icons.

❏ Minimized windows can be restored to full size by clicking on their icon in the Taskbar.

❏ Windows can be arranged on the desktop by pick-ing Cascade or Tile from the Taskbar menu.

❏ A window can be moved about the screen by drag-ging on its title bar.

❏ You can change the size of a window (in Restore mode) by dragging on any of its edges.

❏ The scroll bars will let you move the working area inside a window.

❏ Closing a window closes its program.

4 Exploring folders

The four faces of Explorer

Windows Me has one file management application, but with four very distinct faces. Whichever one you start from, it can be changed into any other by altering the display or by switching the focus between your computer, your network and the Internet.

Windows Explorer (page 46)

This has a dual display, with the folder structure on the left and the contents of the current folder on the right. It can access the folders in all of the drives attached to your computer, and any that may be accessible to you over a network. Windows Explorer is a good tool for moving files between folders.

My Computer (page 47)

This has a simpler display than Explorer. It works in a single-pane window, and when first opened it gives an overview of the components of your own system. You can then open another window to get a detailed look at folders in a drive, and continue opening further windows to go deeper into folders. My Computer only shows the contents of one folder, but you can have as many My Computer windows open as you need.

My Network Places

This is the same as My Computer, but opens with the focus on the networked machines.

Internet Explorer (Chapter 12)

This is the mode for exploring the Internet. The main difference is that it displays Web content – naturally, but this is an option when exploring within your computer – and the toolbar has a slightly different selection of tools.

The jargon

- ❏ Root – the folder of the disk. All other folders branch off from the root.

- ❏ Parent – a folder that contains another.

- ❏ Child – a sub-folder of a Parent.

- ❏ Branch – the structure of sub-folders open off from a folder.

Tip

When planning the folder structure, keep it simple. Too many folders within folders can make it hard to find files.

If you are going to work successfully with Windows Me – or any computer system – you must understand how its disk storage is organised, and how to manage files efficiently and safely. In this chapter, we will look at the filing system, working with folders and the screen displays of Explorer and My Computer. In later sections, we will cover managing files and looking after your disks.

Folders

The hard disks supplied on modern PCs are typically 10 gigabytes or larger. 1 Gigabyte is 1 billion bytes and each byte can hold one character (or part of a number or of a graphic). That means that a typical hard disk can nearly to 2 billion words – enough for about 10,000 hefty novels! More to the point, if you were using it to store letters and reports, it could hold many, many thousands of them. Even if you are storing big audio or video files you are still going to get hundreds of them on the disk. It must be organised if you are ever to find your files.

Folders provide this organisation. They are containers in which related files can be placed to keep them together, and away from other files. A folder can also contain sub-folders – which can themselves by subdivided. You can think of the first level of folders as being sets of filing cabinets; the second level are drawers within the cabinets, and the next level divisions within the drawers. (And these could have subdividers – there is no limit to this.)

Don't just store all your files in My Documents – it will get terribly crowded! Have a separate folder for each type of file, or each area of work (or each user of the computer), subdividing as necessary, so that no folder holds more than a few dozen files.

Paths

The structure of folders is often referred to as the **tree**. It starts at the **root**, which is the drive letter – C: for your main hard disk – and branches off from there.

A folder's position in the tree is described by its **path**. For most operations, you can identify a folder by clicking on it in a screen display, but now and then you will have to type its path. This should start at the drive letter and the root, and include every folder along the branch, with a backslash (\) between the names.

For example:

C:\DTP

C:\WORDPROC\LETTERS

When you want to know a path, look it up in the Explorer display and trace the branches down from the root.

Filenames

A filename has two parts – the name and an extension.

The **name** can be as long as you like, and include almost any characters – including spaces. But don't let the freedom go to your head. The longer the name, the greater the opportunity for typing errors. The most important thing to remember when naming a file is that the name must mean something to you, so that you can find it easily next time you come back to the job.

The **extension** can be from 0 to 3 characters, and is separated from the rest of the name by a dot. It is used to identify the nature of the file. Windows uses the extensions COM, EXE, SYS, INI, DLL to identify special files of its own – handle these with care!

Most applications also use their own special extensions. Word-processor files are often marked with DOC; spreadsheet files are usually XLS; database files typically have DB extensions.

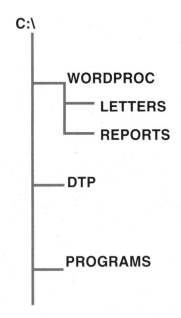

C:\
├── WORDPROC
│   ├── LETTERS
│   └── REPORTS
├── DTP
└── PROGRAMS

Take note

Whatever you call a file, Windows will also give it a name in the old MS-DOS format – which limits the main part to 8 letters – for use with older applications. The name will start with the same six letters, then have ~ (tilde) and a number, e.g. 'LETTER TO BILL.DOC' becomes 'LETTER~1.DOC'.

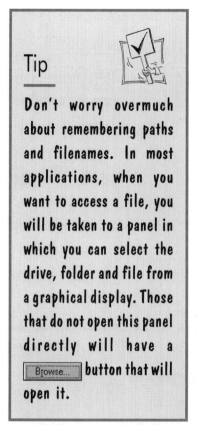

If you are saving a file in a word-processor, spreadsheet or other application, and are asked for a filename, you normally only have to give the first part. The application will take care of the extension. If you do need to give an extension, make it meaningful. BAK is a good extension for backup files; TXT for text files.

When an application asks you for a filename – and the file is in the *current* folder – type in the name and extension only. If the file is in *another* folder, type in the path, a backslash separator and then the filename.

For example:

MYFILE.DOC

C:\WORPROC\REPORTS\MAY25.TXT

A:\MYFILE.BAK

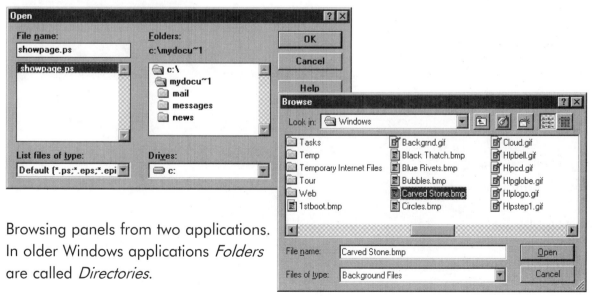

Browsing panels from two applications. In older Windows applications *Folders* are called *Directories*.

45

Windows Explorer

In the Explorer window, the main working area is split, with folders in the Explorer Bar, and the contents on the right.

The **Folders** panel may show the disk drives and first level of folders only, but folders can be expanded to show the sub-folders. (See *Expanding folders*, page 54.)

The **Contents** shows the files and sub-folders in the currently selected folder. These can be displayed as large or small icons accompanied by the name only, or with details of the file's size, type and date it was last modified. (See *Arranging icons*, page 62.) The overall display can be as a Web page (below), or in the Classic style (opposite).

The **Status Bar** shows information about the selected file(s) or folders.

❑ Starting Explorer

1 Click 🏁 Start .

2 Point to Programs then to Accessories.

3 Click Windows Explorer.

4 Click on a folder's icon 📁 or its name to open 📂 it and display its contents.

When viewed as a Web page, a description of the selected file is shown here

Click to close the Explorer Bar   Contents

Explorer Bar, displaying Folders

Current folder

Root

First level folder

Sub-folder

Status Bar

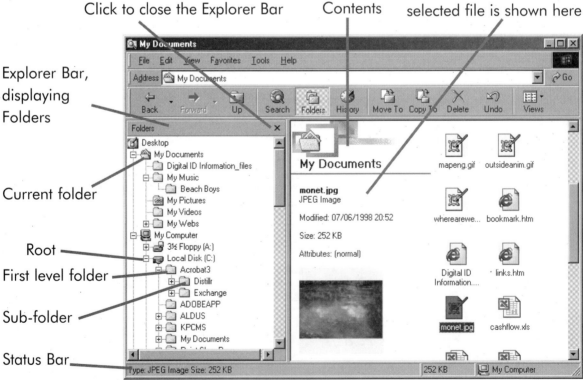

46

The Standard toolbar

- ❏ Navigation
- ⬅ Go back to previous folder
- ➡ Go to next folder
- 🔼 Go to parent folder
- ❏ Explorer Bar
- 🔍 Search for files (page 70)
- 📁 Favorites (page 168)
- 🕐 History (page 167)
- ❏ Manage files
- 📂 Move To Folder
- 📋 Copy To Folder
- ✖ Delete file or folder
- ↩ Undo last action
- ▦ Alternative views of files (page 52)

At its default settings, the display of My Computer is simple, uncluttered and quite effective. You can see at a glance what files and folders are in the current folder – as long as there aren't too many! But sometimes, you need more control and more information.

The Toolbar has tools for all common tasks, plus a (limited) means of changing folders. The folder list on the Toolbar only shows the drives and the folders in the path from the root to the current one.

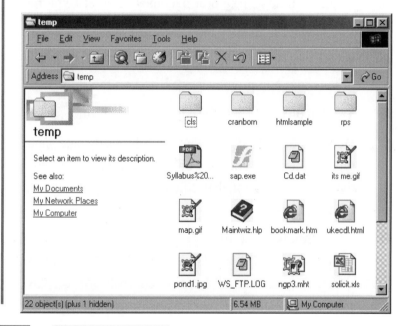

Tip

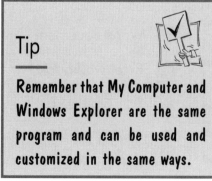

Remember that My Computer and Windows Explorer are the same program and can be used and customized in the same ways.

Use the drop-down list to switch to drives or folders higher up the same path

Display options

The display options can be set from the View menu and the Views button. These options can be set at any time, and can be different for different folders. There are two areas of choice.

Which toolbars to you want?

- The **Standard** is pretty well essential.

- The **Address** is useful. Its drop-down outline of the folder structure offers a quick way to move between drives.

- The **Links** and **Radio** are only for on-line use – turn these on and Windows Explorer becomes Internet Explorer.

How do you want to display the files?

- With **Large icons** it is easier to see the type of files – some of the more common ones are listed on the right.

- **Small icons** and **List** show lots of files in little space.

- **Details** are useful if you want to find files by date, size or type. In this view you can click on a column header to list the files in order of that column – and click again for inverse order.

- **Thumbnails** show little previews of files, if possible. Graphics and Web pages will normally be displayed, Word, PowerPoint and Excel documents will display if they were saved with the preview option turned on.

Tip

There's more on arranging files in the next chapter.

Basic steps

- ❑ Displaying Toolbars
1 Open the View menu.
2 Point to Toolbars then click on a toolbar to turn it on or off.

- ❑ Icons and lists
3 Open the View menu.
or
4 Click ▣ Views ▾.
5 Choose a view.

Common file icons

 Audio/Video file

 Bitmap

 Graphic (GIF/JPG)

 Help file

 Web page

 Text

 Word document

 Excel workbook

 TrueType font

 System file – handle with care!

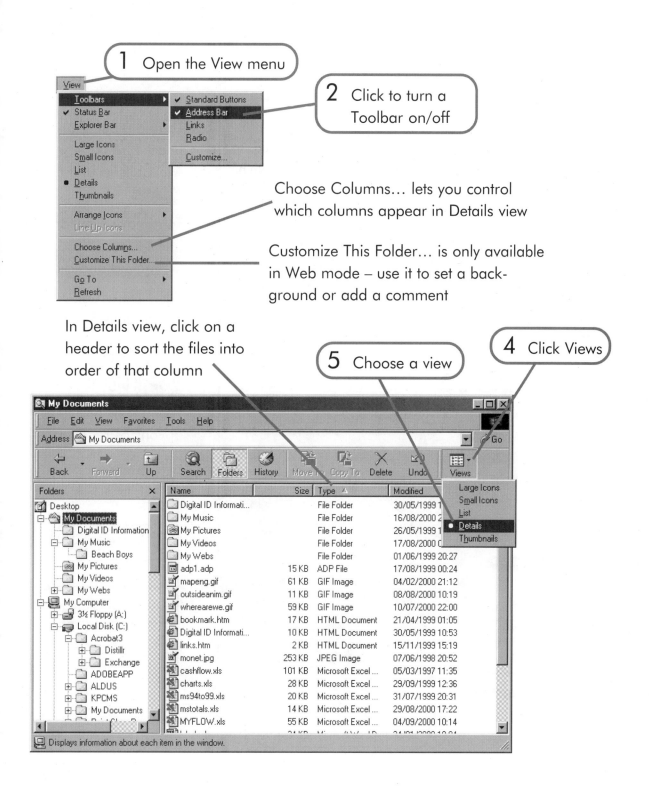

1 Open the View menu

2 Click to turn a Toolbar on/off

Choose Columns... lets you control which columns appear in Details view

Customize This Folder... is only available in Web mode – use it to set a background or add a comment

In Details view, click on a header to sort the files into order of that column

5 Choose a view

4 Click Views

49

Customizing the toolbar

The contents of the Standard toolbar are not fixed. You can add or remove buttons, move them around within the bar, and adjust their appearance. This is all done through the **Customize Toolbar** dialog box.

There are buttons available for most of the other commands in the menus, including Edit – Cut, Copy and Paste. These can be used for copying and moving files and folders, instead of dragging or using the Move To/Copy To routines (see page 67).

1 Right-click on the toolbar and select Customize…

2 To add a button, select it from the Available list and click Add ->.

3 To remove a button, select it from the Current list and click <- Remove.

4 To adjust its position, select it and click Move Up (left) or Move Down (right).

5 Set the Text and Icon options as required.

6 Click Close.

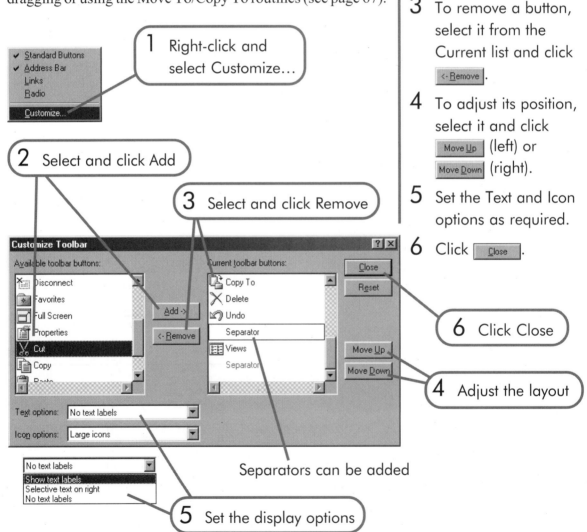

1 Right-click and select Customize…

2 Select and click Add

3 Select and click Remove

6 Click Close

4 Adjust the layout

Separators can be added

5 Set the display options

50

Single window browsing

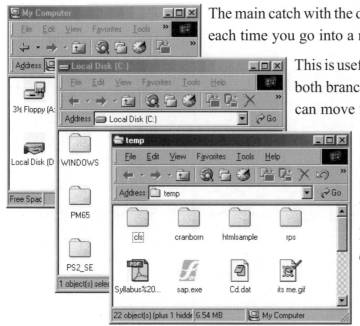

The main catch with the default settings in My Computer is that each time you go into a new folder, it opens another window.

This is useful if you want to open two folders, that both branch off from a previous one, so that you can move files from one to the other.

It can be a nuisance, however, if you want to travel down the line to a third or fourth level folder. The screen clogs up with unwanted windows.

My Computer can be made to open each new folder in the same window.

There are two ways to do this:

● Hold down the **[Ctrl]** key when you click to open a new folder.

● Go to the **Folder Options** and select *Open each folder in the same window* (see page 52).

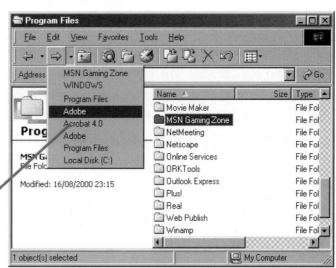

In single-window browsing the drop-down list on the Back button gives you quick access to the folders opened on the way down to the current one.

Once you have gone back, the Forward button and drop-down list also become active.

Folder Options

These control the overall appearance of folders and the way that files are handled. The dialog box has three tabs.

The **General** tab set the basic nature of folder displays and the way things are selected – not just in Windows Explorer and but My Computer, but also on the Desktop. You can set folders to look like Web pages, with links to files and folders underlined and responding to a single click, or have the 'classic' displays, where you click once to select and double-click to activate. A combination of the two is also possible. This tab is also where you can set the option to open each folder in a new or in the same window.

The **View** panel controls the display of files. There are two main options here. The first is whether to show 'hidden' files. These are mainly found in the *Windows* and *Windows/System* folders and are ones that you do not usually need to see and which are safer out of the way.

- **Application extensions** – files with **.DLL** extensions. They are used by applications and must not be deleted.

- **System files** – marked by **.SYS** after the name. These are essential to Windows Me's internal workings.

- **Drivers** – with **.VXD** or **.DRV** extensions. These make printers, screens and other hardware work properly.

The second key choice is whether you want set different display styles for different folders – turn on *Remember each folder's view settings* if you do. If you have a mixture of styles already and want all folders to look the same, you can use the buttons to make them all look like the current folder or reset them all to their default settings.

The **File Types** panel is used to link programs and documents. We'll come back to this on page 76.

1 Open the Tools menu and select Folder Options...

2 On the General panel select Web or Classic style for the Desktop.

3 Select Web or Classic style for the folders.

4 Set the Browse Folders option – the same or a new window?

5 Set the Click option.

6 Go to the View panel.

7 Click the checkbox to turn options on or off.

8 Click ⬚Apply⬚ to test the effect.

9 When you have done. click ⬚OK⬚.

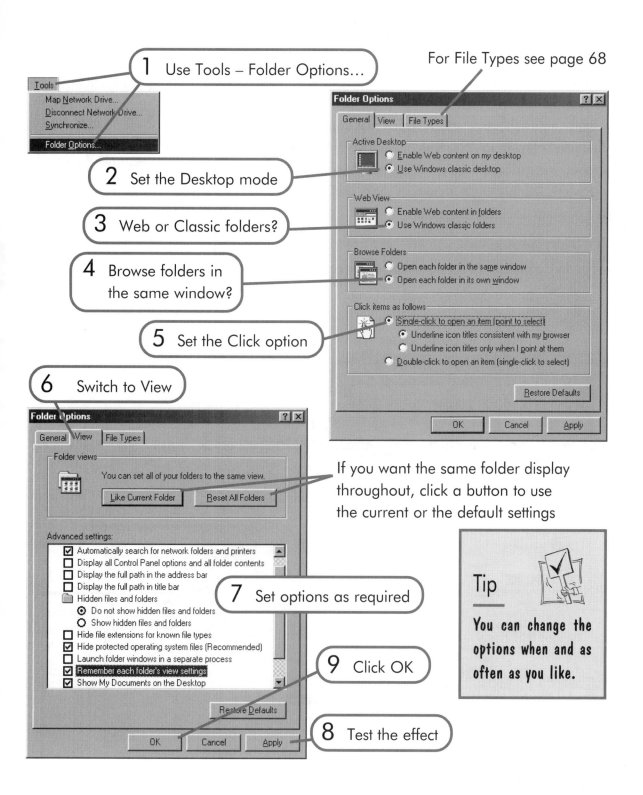

1 Use Tools – Folder Options...

For File Types see page 68

Tools
Map Network Drive...
Disconnect Network Drive...
Synchronize...
Folder Options...

Folder Options ? X

General | View | File Types

2 Set the Desktop mode

Active Desktop
○ Enable Web content on my desktop
● Use Windows classic desktop

3 Web or Classic folders?

Web View
○ Enable Web content in folders
● Use Windows classic folders

4 Browse folders in the same window?

Browse Folders
○ Open each folder in the same window
● Open each folder in its own window

5 Set the Click option

Click items as follows
● Single-click to open an item (point to select)
  ● Underline icon titles consistent with my browser
  ○ Underline icon titles only when I point at them
○ Double-click to open an item (single-click to select)

Restore Defaults

6 Switch to View

OK | Cancel | Apply

Folder Options ? X

General | View | File Types

Folder views
You can set all of your folders to the same view.

Like Current Folder | Reset All Folders

If you want the same folder display throughout, click a button to use the current or the default settings

Advanced settings:
☑ Automatically search for network folders and printers
☐ Display all Control Panel options and all folder contents
☐ Display the full path in the address bar
☐ Display the full path in title bar
📁 Hidden files and folders
  ⊙ Do not show hidden files and folders
  ○ Show hidden files and folders
☐ Hide file extensions for known file types
☑ Hide protected operating system files (Recommended)
☐ Launch folder windows in a separate process
☑ Remember each folder's view settings
☑ Show My Documents on the Desktop

7 Set options as required

9 Click OK

Restore Defaults

OK | Cancel | Apply

8 Test the effect

Tip

You can change the options when and as often as you like.

Expanding folders

The *Folders* structure can be shown in outline form, or with some or all of its branches shown in full. The best display is always the simplest one that will show you all you need. This usually means that most of the structure is collapsed back to its first level of main folders, with one or two branches expanded to show particular sub-folders. It is sometimes worth expanding the whole lot, just to get an idea of the overall structure and to see how sub-folders fit together.

If a folder has sub-folders, it will have a symbol beside it.

+ has sub-folders, and can be expanded

− sub-folders displayed and can be collapsed.

❏ To expand a folder

1 Click ⊞ by its name.

2 Click ⊞ by any sub-folders if you want to fully expand the whole branching set.

❏ To collapse a folder

3 Click ⊟ by its name.

❏ To collapse a whole branch

4 Click ⊟ by the folder at the top of the branched set.

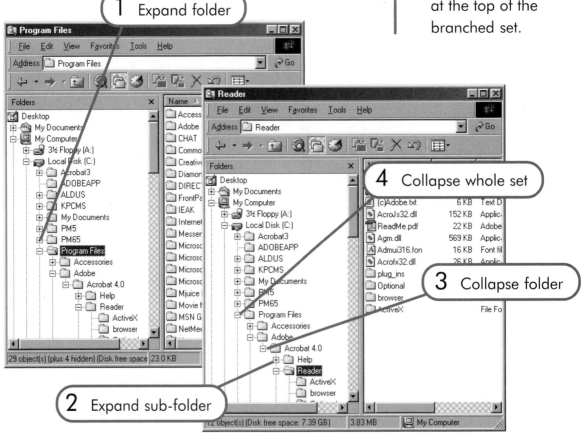

1 Expand folder

4 Collapse whole set

3 Collapse folder

2 Expand sub-folder

Basic steps

1 Point to the folder name and click the right mouse button.

2 Select Properties from the short menu.

3 Wait for for the system to work out the total space and number of files.

4 Click ⊠ to close the Properties panel.

Folder properties

Expanding a folder will show you what is in it, but not how much space all its files and sub-folders occupy. The space report in the Status bar tells you how much is used by the files in the current folder only – not in its sub-folders. The total space figure can be important if you want to back up the folder, or copy it to floppies. The Properties panel will tell us this – and other things.

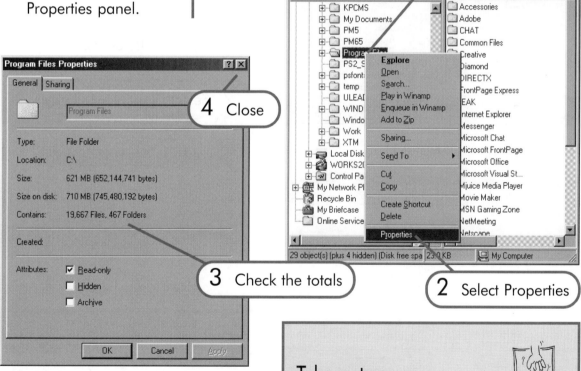

The size of the disk space they occupy is more than the size of the files, because some space is left empty but unusable at the ends of files and around small ones.

Take note

You can right-click almost everything to see its Properties and find out more about the item.

Creating a folder

Organised people set up their folders before they need them, so that they have places to store their letters – private and business, reports, memos, notes, and whatever, when they start to write them on their new system. They have a clear idea of the structure that they want, and create their folders at the right branches.

1 Select the folder that will be the parent of your new one, or the root if you want a new first-level folder.

2 Open the File menu and point to New then select Folder.

3 Replace 'New Folder' with a new name – any length, any characters as with filenames.

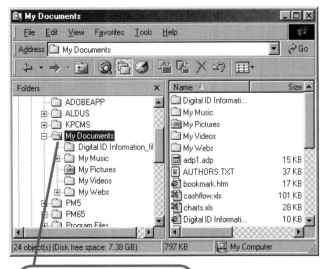

1 Click on the parent

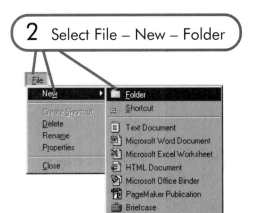

2 Select File – New – Folder

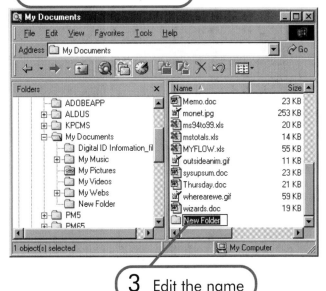

3 Edit the name

Tip

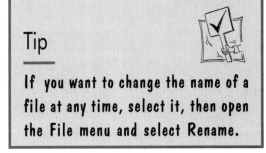

If you want to change the name of a file at any time, select it, then open the File menu and select Rename.

Your folder structure

How you organise your folders is entirely up to you, but these guidelines may help.

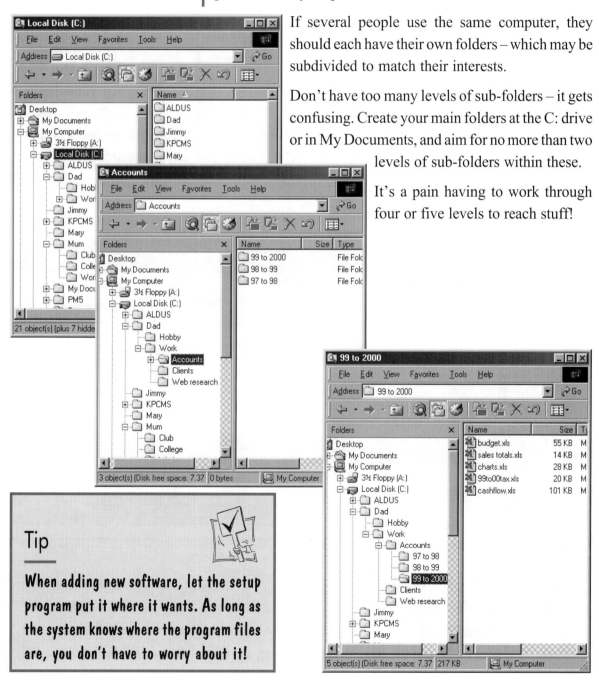

If several people use the same computer, they should each have their own folders – which may be subdivided to match their interests.

Don't have too many levels of sub-folders – it gets confusing. Create your main folders at the C: drive or in My Documents, and aim for no more than two levels of sub-folders within these.

It's a pain having to work through four or five levels to reach stuff!

Tip

When adding new software, let the setup program put it where it wants. As long as the system knows where the program files are, you don't have to worry about it!

Moving folders

Those of us who are less organised set up our new folders when the old ones get so full that it is difficult to find things. Nor do we always create them in the most suitable place in the tree. Fortunately, Windows Me caters for us too. Files can easily be moved from one folder to another (see *Moving and copying*, page 66), and folders can easily be moved to new places on the tree.

In this example, *graphics* is being moved from within My Documents to become a top level folder on Drive C:.

1 Arrange the display so that you can see the folder you want to move and the place it has to move to.

2 Drag the folder to its new position – the target folder will be highlighted when you are in the right place.

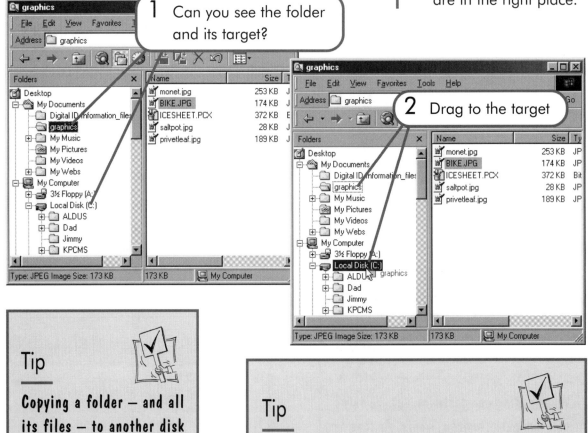

Tip

Copying a folder – and all its files – to another disk can be a quick way to make a backup of a set of files.

Tip

If you can't get the original and target folders in the same display, use Edit – Move To Folder, see page 67.

Deleting folders

1 Select the folder.

2 Check the files list. Are
   there any there? Do
   you want any of them?
   No, carry on.

3 Right-click on the
   folder to open the
   context menu or open
   the File menu and
   select Delete.

4 If necessary, you can
   stop the process by
   clicking No when you
   are asked to confirm
   that the folder is to be
   thrown in the Bin.

This is not something you will do every day, for deleting a
folder also deletes its files, and files are usually precious things.
But we all acquire programs we don't need, keep files long past
their use-by dates, and sometimes create unnecessary folders.

● Don't worry about accidental deletions – files and folders
   deleted from your hard disk can be restored thanks to the
   Recycle Bin. (See page 69.)

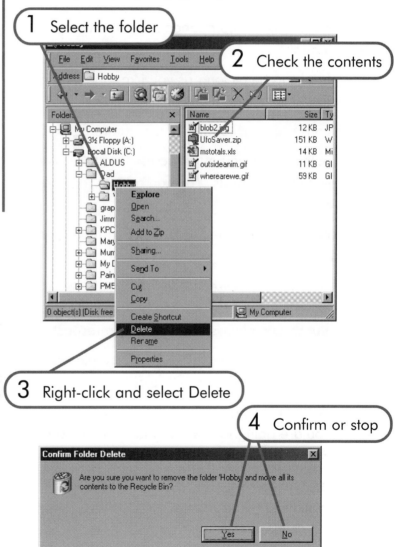

1 Select the folder

2 Check the contents

3 Right-click and select Delete

4 Confirm or stop

Tip

You can also delete folders
– and files – by dragging
them directly to the Recycle Bin (see page 69).

Summary

❑ Windows Explorer and My Computer are two faces of the same program and are used for managing your files and folders.

❑ Disks are normally subdivided into folders, to give organised storage for files.

❑ A folder's place in the system is identified by its path.

❑ A filename has two components, the name itself and an extension.

❑ The name can be as long as you like, and contain any mixture of letters, digits and symbols.

❑ Extensions are used to identify the nature of the file.

❑ The Toolbar gives you quick access to all the commonly-used commands. You can add or remove buttons as required.

❑ You can control the file displays through the Folder options.

❑ Those files that are essential to the system are usually hidden from view. They can be brought into view, but should always be treated with respect.

❑ When you create a new folder, it will be placed on the branch below the selected folder.

❑ Try to keep your folder structure as simple as possible – you are going to have to find your way around your system!

❑ A folder, and its files, can be deleted or moved to a new position in the structure.

5 Managing files

Arranging icons

Unless you specify otherwise, the Contents display lists your folders and files in alphabetical order – icons arranged across the screen; lists arranged in columns. Most of the time this works fine, but when you are moving or copying files, or hunting for them, other arrangements can be more convenient.

Basic steps

1 Open the View menu and point to Arrange Icons.

2 Select by Name, Type, Size or Date.

❑ Details View

3 Open the View menu and select Details.

4 To sort by Name, Size, Type or Date, click on the column header. Click twice to sort into reverse order.

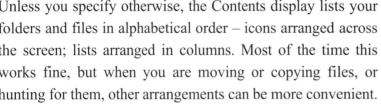

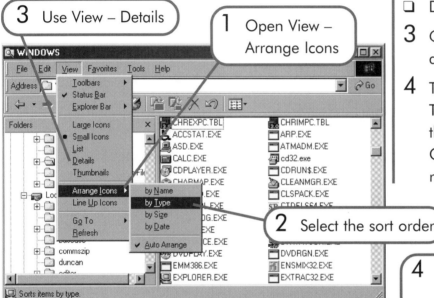

3 Use View – Details

1 Open View – Arrange Icons

2 Select the sort order

4 Click the header to sort on that column

Tip

If you need to free up some disk space and are looking for files to delete, use the Details display and arrange the icons by Size or by Date to bring the biggest or oldest together.

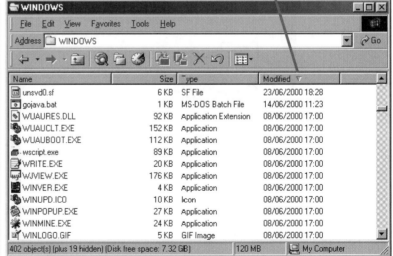

Improving visibility

❑ Adjusting Details

1 Point the cursor at the dividing line between two field headings.

2 When the cursor changes to ✚, drag the dividing line to change the width of the field on its left.

❑ Adjusting the split

3 Point anywhere on the bar between the panes to get the ✚ cursor.

4 Drag the shadowed line to adjust the relative size of the panes.

The amount of information in a My Computer or Windows Explorer display can vary greatly, depending upon the number of items in a folder and the display style. You should be able to adjust the display so that you can see things properly.

As well as being able to set the overall size of the window, you can also adjust the width of each field in a Details display, and the split between the Folders and Contents panes of Explorer.

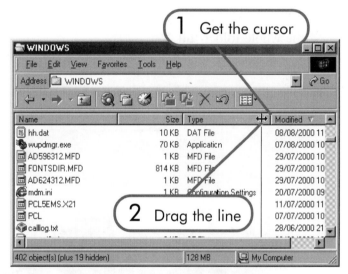

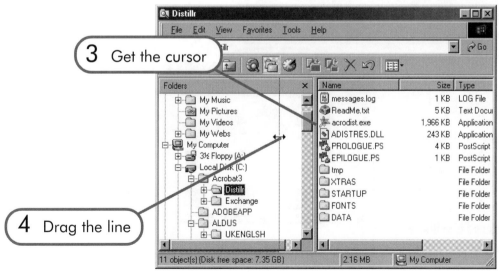

Selecting sets of files

You can easily select single files by clicking on them, but you can also select groups of files. This is useful when you want to back up a day's work by copying the new files to a floppy disk, or move a group from one folder to another, or delete a load of files that are not wanted.

You can select:

● a block of adjacent files;

● a scattered set;

● the whole folder-full.

The same techniques work with all display styles.

❑ To select a block using the mouse

1 Point to one corner of the block and click.

2 Hold down the mouse button and drag an outline around the ones you want.

❑ [Shift] selecting

3 Click on the file at one end of the block.

4 If necessary, scroll the window to bring the other end into view.

5 Hold [Shift].

6 Click on the far end file.

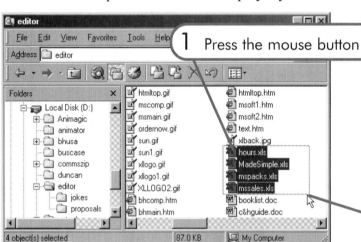

1 Press the mouse button

2 Drag to enclose

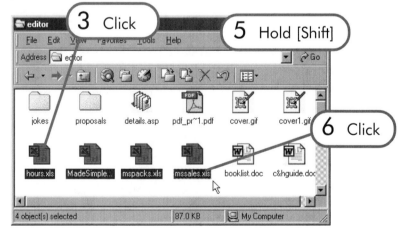

3 Click

5 Hold [Shift]

6 Click

Tip

Small icons and List views are best for these jobs!

Basic steps

❏ To select scattered files

1 Click on any one of the files you want.

2 Hold [Ctrl] and click each of the other files.

❏ You can deselect any file by clicking on it a second time.

❏ To select all the files

3 Open the Edit menu.

4 Choose Select All.

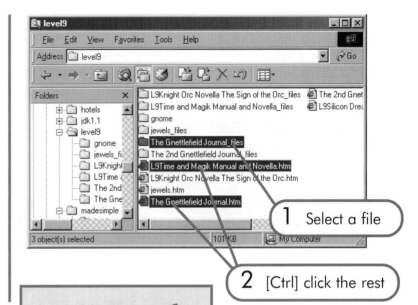

1 Select a file

2 [Ctrl] click the rest

Tip

It may be easier to arrange icons by Name, Date or Type, and [Shift] select.

3 Open the Edit menu

4 Choose Select All

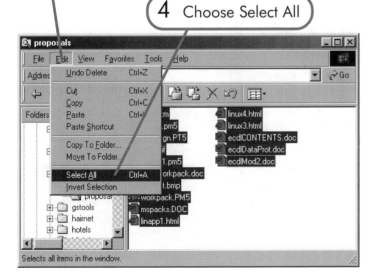

Tip

If you want all the files except for a scattered few, select those few, then use Edit – Invert Selection to deselect them and select the others.

Moving and copying

When you drag a file from one place to another, it will either move or copy the file. In general:

- It is a **move** if you drag to somewhere *on the same disk.*
- It is a **copy** if you drag the file *to a different disk.*

When you are dragging files within a disk, you are usually moving to reorganise your storage; and copying is most commonly used to create a safe backup on a separate disk.

If you want to move a file from one disk to another, or copy within a disk, hold down the right mouse button while you drag. A menu will appear when you reach the target folder. You can select Move or Copy from there.

1 Select the file(s).

2 Scroll the Folders list so that you can see the target folder — don't click on it!

3 Point to any one of the selected files and drag to the target.

or

4 Hold down the right mouse button while you drag then select Move or Copy.

❑ Quick copy to a floppy

5 Right-click on the file to open its context menu, point to Send To and select the floppy drive.

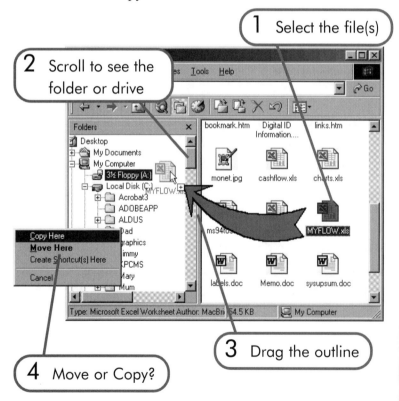

1 Select the file(s)

2 Scroll to see the folder or drive

3 Drag the outline

4 Move or Copy?

5 Send the file to a floppy

Basic steps

Move To Folder/Copy To Folder

1 Select the file(s).

2 Open the Edit menu and select Copy To or Move To Folder.

Or

3 Click Copy To or Move To Folder.

4 Select the target drive or folder.

5 Click ▮ OK ▮.

If you are having difficulty arranging the Explorer display so that you can see the source files and the target folder, the simplest approach is to use the **Move To Folder** or **Copy To Folder** commands. These let you pick the target folder through a dialog box.

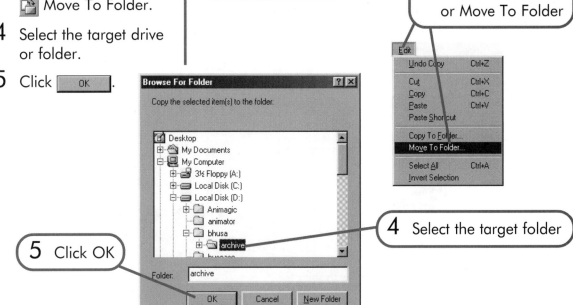

1 Select the file(s)

2 Use Edit – Copy To or Move To Folder

4 Select the target folder

5 Click OK

Cut and Paste

Windows Me allows you to move and copy files and folders – or any other data, through an area of memory called the Clipboard (see page 158).

Cut, **Copy** and **Paste** are on the **Edit** menu of all Windows applications.

Copy stores a copy of the file or folder in the Clipboard.

Cut removes the original file, storing a copy in the Clipboard.

Paste puts a copy of the stored file into the current folder.

Deleting files

Thanks to the Recycle Bin, deleting files is no longer the dangerous occupation that it used to be – up to a point! Anything that you delete from the hard disk goes first into the Bin, from which it can easily be recovered. Floppies are different. If you delete a file from a floppy it really does get wiped out!

1 Select the file, or group of files.

2 Drag them to the Recycle Bin on the Desktop or in Explorer.

or

3 Press [Delete].

4 At the Confirm prompt, click Yes or No to confirm or stop the deletion.

1 Select the files

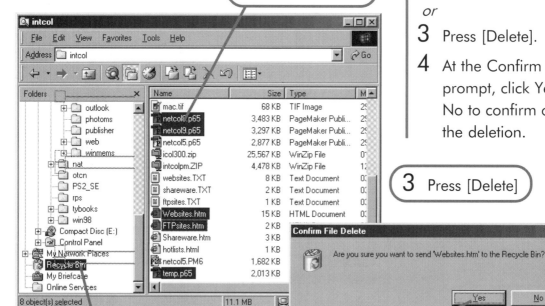

3 Press [Delete]

2 Drag to the Bin

4 Confirm

Take note

If you want to rename a file, select it and use File – Rename, or click twice, separately, on the filename to highlight it. The name can then be edited or retyped.

With single deletions, the filename is displayed; with multiple deletions you just get the number of selected files.

Basic steps

Recycle Bin

1 Open the Recycle Bin from the icon on the desktop or from Windows Explorer.

2 Select the files that were deleted by mistake – the Original Location field shows you where they were.

3 Right-click for the Context menu or open the File menu and select Restore.

This is a wonderful feature, especially for those of us given to making instant decisions that we later regret. Until you empty the Bin, any 'deleted' files and folders can be instantly restored – and if the folder that they were stored in has also been deleted, that is re-created first, so things go back into their proper place.

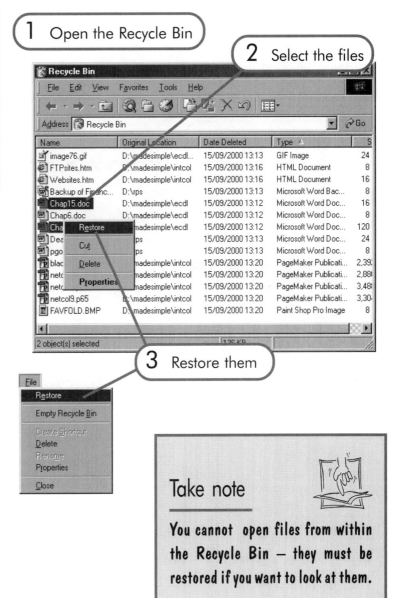

1 Open the Recycle Bin

2 Select the files

3 Restore them

Tip

Files sent to the Recycle Bin stay there until you empty it. Do this regularly, to free up disk space. Check that there is nothing that you want (Restore any files if necessary) then use File – Empty Recycle Bin.

Take note

You cannot open files from within the Recycle Bin – they must be restored if you want to look at them.

Finding files

If you are well organised, have a clear and logical structure of folders and consistently store your files in their proper places, then you should rarely need this facility when hunting outside your system. However, if you belong to the other 90% of users, you will be grateful for it.

● Find can track down files by name, type, age, size or contents. As long as you have something to go on, no files need remain lost for long.

● You can start a search from Explorer or the Start menu.

Basic steps

❑ Finding by name

1 From Explorer, open the View menu, point to Explorer Bar and select Search.

or

2 Click on Start, point to Search and select Files or Folders...

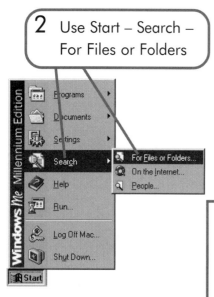

2 Use Start – Search – For Files or Folders

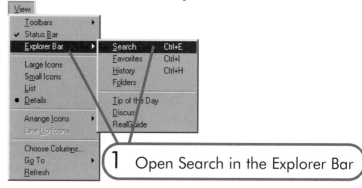

1 Open Search in the Explorer Bar

Take note

The other Search options are for finding people or files on the Internet.

Partial names and wildcards

If you type part of a name into the Named box, the Search will track down any file with those characters anywhere in the name.

e.g. 'DOC' will find 'My Documents', 'Letter to doctor', and all Word files with a .DOC extension.

If you know the start of the name and the extension, fill the gap with the wildcard *. (include the dot!)

e.g. *REP*.TXT* will find 'REPORT MAY 15.*TXT*', 'REPLY TO IRS.TXT' and similar files.

3   Type as much of the name as you know into the Named slot.

4   If the file can be identified by special words enter them in the Containing text box.

5   Select the drive from the Look in list.

6   Click Search Now.

7   Double-click the file to run it or to open it with its linked program.

If you cannot remember a file's name, you may be able to find it by its Date, Type, Size or other features. Tick a checkbox to reveal the settings for the option then define it.

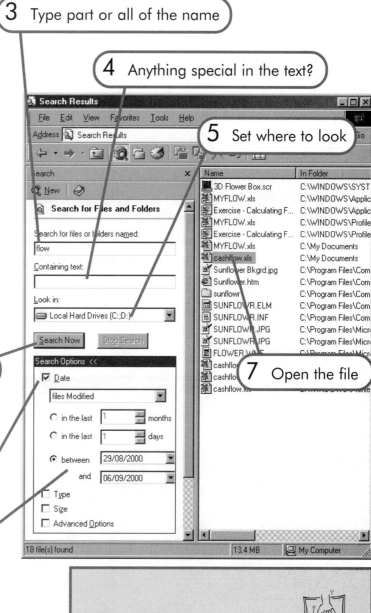

3   Type part or all of the name

4   Anything special in the text?

5   Set where to look

6   Start the search

7   Open the file

Take note

You can also print, delete and otherwise manage a found file through options on the File menu.

Properties

As we saw on page 8, everything in Windows Me has Properties. If you open the Properties box for any file, you will see a General panel, containing information about the file and some controls. Some files have additional panels.

● Program files have Version panels carrying product details;

● Word-processor, spreadsheet and other data files created by newer applications have Summary and Statistics panels. Summary information is created by the application's user to describe the contents of the file; the Statistics include the number of pages, words, characters and the like, and the dates when the file was created, last modified or accessed.

● Shortcuts have their own special panels (see next pages).

Basic steps

1 Select the file and click the 🗒 toolbar button.

or

2 Right-click the file and select Properties from the short menu.

3 If you want to prevent the file from being edited, tick the Read Only checkbox.

4 Click tabs to open other panels, if present.

5 Click [OK] or [x] to close.

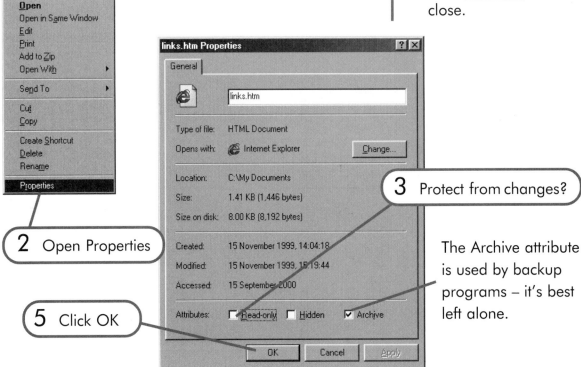

2 Open Properties

5 Click OK

3 Protect from changes?

The Archive attribute is used by backup programs – it's best left alone.

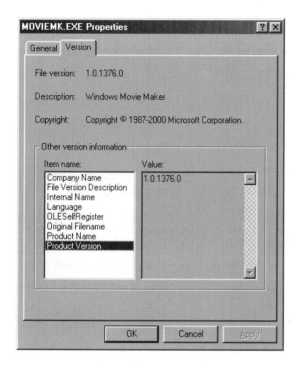

The Version panel (left) can tell you more about when and by whom a program was created. As its name implies, it is particularly useful for checking which version of a program you have.

The Summary panel (below) displays information written into it while the file was open in its application. This can be edited – click Apply or OK to save the revised information.

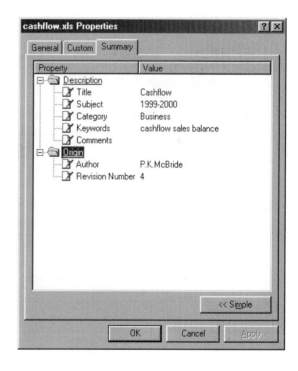

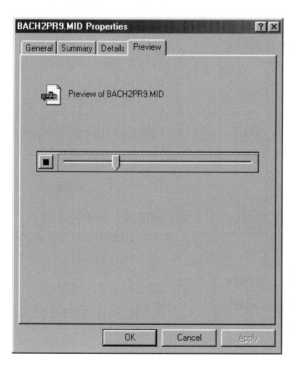

Some files will have Preview panels where you can see – or listen to – the contents.

Shortcuts

You can run a program by double-clicking on its EXE file in Explorer or My Computer, but Shortcuts make it easier. Shortcuts can be added to the Start menu (see page 86) or placed directly on the Desktop. This is a very convenient way of running programs that you use regularly.

Most programs will have shortcuts set up in the Start menu, and sometimes on the Desktop, when they are installed. If not, or you want extra ones, you can set up a shortcut in a minute – and if you don't make much use of it, you can remove it even faster!

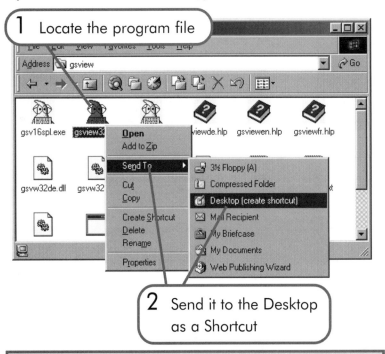

1 Locate the program file

2 Send it to the Desktop as a Shortcut

Take note

Too many shortcuts will clutter up your Desktop. Remove excess ones by selecting them and pressing [Delete]. This does not remove the program – only the shortcut.

Basic steps

1 Find the program file – it will have an EXE or COM extension.

2 Right-click on the file and select Send To then Desktop as Shortcut from its context menu.

or

3 Put the Explorer window into Restore mode so you can see some Desktop.

4 Hold down the right mouse button and drag the program icon onto the Desktop.

5 Release the button and select Create shortcut here.

6 Edit the name – it will be 'Shortcut to...'

❑ Editing Properties

7 Open the icon's Properties box and click the Shortcut tab.

8 Change the Start in folder if required.

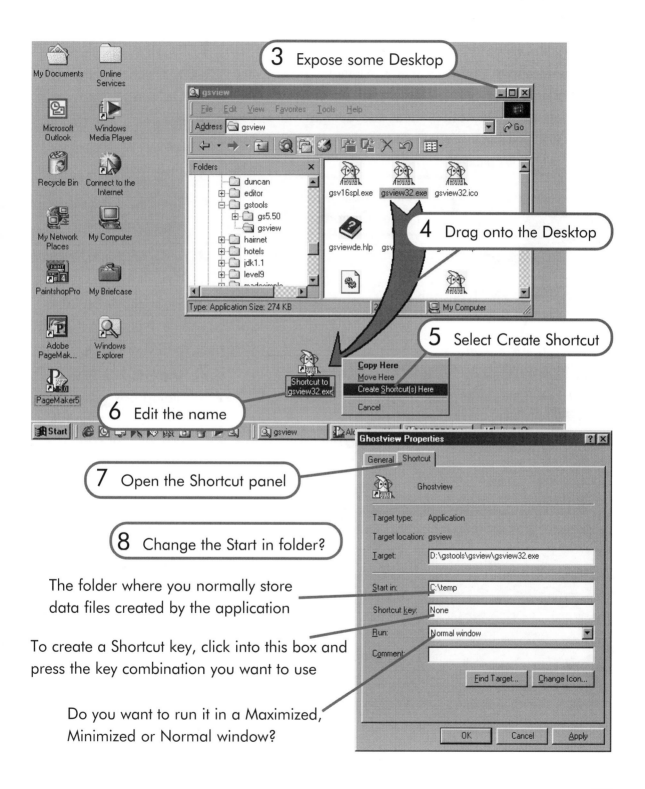

3 Expose some Desktop

4 Drag onto the Desktop

5 Select Create Shortcut

6 Edit the name

7 Open the Shortcut panel

8 Change the Start in folder?

The folder where you normally store
data files created by the application

To create a Shortcut key, click into this box and
press the key combination you want to use

Do you want to run it in a Maximized,
Minimized or Normal window?

File Types

Windows Me keeps a list of registered file types. These are ones that it knows how to describe and how to handle. If you open a document of a known type, the system will run the appropriate application and load in the file. Windows Me comes with a good long list, and you can teach it about new types through one of the Folder Options panels.

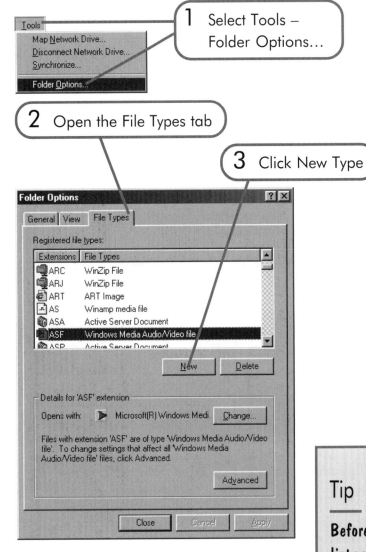

1 Select Tools –
Folder Options...

2 Open the File Types tab

3 Click New Type

Basic steps

1 Open the Tools menu and select Folder Options...

2 Go to the File Types tab.

3 Click ⬚ New ⬚.

4 Enter the Extension that marks this type.

5 Click ⬚ Advanced >> ⬚ to open the full box.

6 Select the Associated File Type from the list and click ⬚ OK ⬚.

7 The Edit File Type dialog box will open for you to define the actions that can be performed on this file. Click ⬚ New... ⬚.

8 In the Action slot, type '*open*'.

9 Click ⬚ Browse... ⬚ and find the application to use, then click ⬚ OK ⬚.

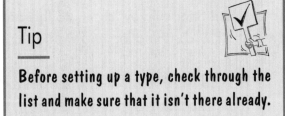

Tip

Before setting up a type, check through the list and make sure that it isn't there already.

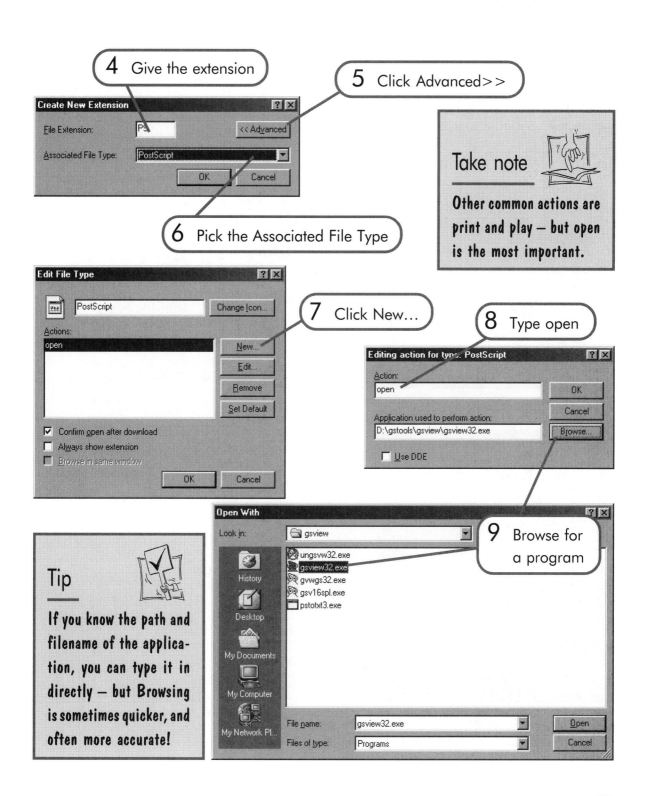

4 Give the extension

5 Click Advanced>>

Create New Extension

File Extension: PS

<< Advanced

Associated File Type: PostScript

OK   Cancel

6 Pick the Associated File Type

Take note

Other common actions are print and play – but open is the most important.

Edit File Type

PostScript   Change Icon...

Actions:

open

New...
Edit...
Remove
Set Default

☑ Confirm open after download
☐ Always show extension
☐ Browse in same window

OK   Cancel

7 Click New...

8 Type open

Editing action for type: PostScript

Action:

open

OK
Cancel

Application used to perform action:

D:\gstools\gsview\gsview32.exe   Browse...

☐ Use DDE

Tip

If you know the path and filename of the application, you can type it in directly – but Browsing is sometimes quicker, and often more accurate!

Open With

Look in: gsview

History
Desktop
My Documents
My Computer
My Network Pl...

ungsvw32.exe
gsview32.exe
gvwgs32.exe
gsv16spl.exe
pstotxt3.exe

9 Browse for a program

File name: gsview32.exe   Open

Files of type: Programs   Cancel

Open With...

The Folder Options File Type tab offers a thorough, if long-winded, means of registering new types. A simpler alternative is to wait until you come across unknown types of file, and use the Open With routine to tell Windows which programs to use.

❑ Opening With ...

1 Right-click on a file to get its context menu. If the first item is Open, Windows knows how to handle it – stop now!

2 Select Open With...

3 At the Open With dialog box, type a Description. This will be used in Details displays in Explorer.

4 Scroll through the list and pick the program to use with this file.

5 If you can't find the program in the list click Other... and browse through your folders to find it.

6 Tick the Always use this program box, if relevant – sometimes you may want to use the same file with different programs.

7 Click OK.

2 Select Open With...

- **Open**
- Add to Zip
- Open With...
- Send To ▶
- Cut
- Copy
- Create Shortcut
- Delete
- Rename
- Properties

> ## Tip
>
> **Free (or cheap) programs to handle almost all types of files are available on the Internet. One of the best stores is at:**
>
> http://www.shareware.com

3 Give a description

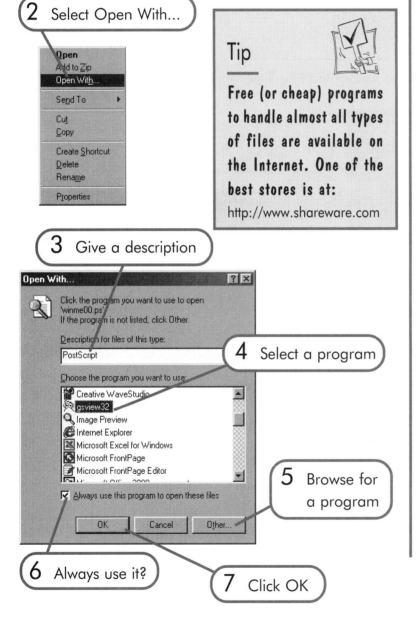

4 Select a program

5 Browse for a program

6 Always use it?

7 Click OK

Basic steps

1 Open the Folder
  Options box and go to
  the File Types tab.

❑ To change a link

2 Select the extension.

3 Click Change... .

4 Pick the application
  and click OK .

❑ To remove a link

5 Select the extension
  and click Delete .

Editing a type

Whether you set up your new type through the Folder Options, or through Open With, you may need to change things later. Some programs will claim for themselves file types that you would prefer to link to a different program, and established file types may also need editing over time as you replace programs with newer versions, but still retain the data files.

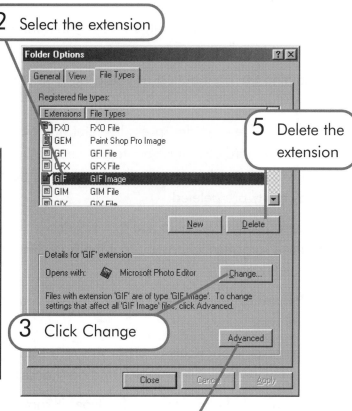

2 Select the extension

5 Delete the extension

3 Click Change

4 Pick a new program

The Advanced button takes you through to the Edit File Type dialog box to change the way all files of that type are handled – see page 77

Take note

Every time you open the File Types panel, Windows Me scans your system to pick up all the links between programs and files – expect to wait for a few seconds.

Summary

❑ You can arrange icons by Name, Type, Size or Date.

❑ Files and folders can be displayed as icons or in lists with details.

❑ You can use [Shift] to select a block of files, or [Ctrl] to select a scattered set. A block of files can also be selected with the mouse.

❑ Dragging a file will normally move it within the disk, or copy it to a floppy.

❑ By holding the right button as you drag, you can copy within a disk or move to a floppy.

❑ To delete a file or folder, press [Delete]. If the file was on the hard disk, it is sent to the Recycle Bin, from which it can be recovered. Files deleted from a floppy really are deleted.

❑ The Search utility will help you to track down files if you have forgotten where you put them, or what they were called.

❑ The Properties box of a file can be a useful source of information.

❑ You can create Shortcuts to programs and place them on your Desktop for quick and easy access.

❑ If Windows Me knows about a file type, it knows how to describe it and what program to open it with. You can teach the system about new types.

❑ When you try to open a file of an unknown type, you will get the Open With... option and can then tell it which program to use.

6 The Taskbar

Taskbar options

Many parts of the Windows Me system can be tailored to your own tastes. Some of the most important are covered in the next two chapters. We'll start with the Taskbar and the Start menu. You can adjust the size of the menu icons, turn the clock on or off, hide the Taskbar, or place it on any edge of the screen.

Basic steps

❑ Adjusting the display

1 Click **Start**.

2 Point to Settings.

3 Click on Taskbar & Start Menu...

4 Set an option.

5 Click **Apply** to see how it looks.

6 Click **OK** to fix the settings and close.

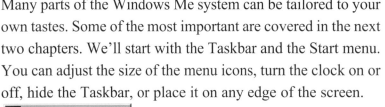

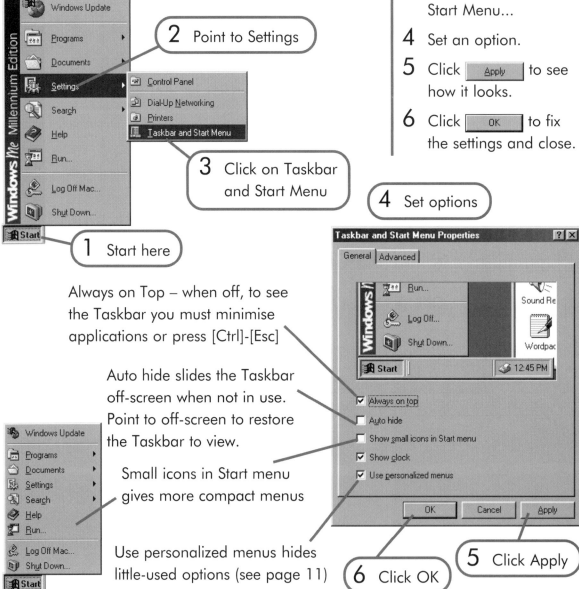

2 Point to Settings

3 Click on Taskbar and Start Menu

1 Start here

4 Set options

Always on Top – when off, to see the Taskbar you must minimise applications or press [Ctrl]-[Esc]

Auto hide slides the Taskbar off-screen when not in use. Point to off-screen to restore the Taskbar to view.

Small icons in Start menu gives more compact menus

Use personalized menus hides little-used options (see page 11)

5 Click Apply

6 Click OK

Moving and resizing

❑ Moving

1 Point to any free space on the Taskbar.

2 Drag towards the top, left or right of the screen, as desired.

3 Release the mouse button.

❑ Resizing

4 Point to the inside edge of the Taskbar.

5 When the cursor changes to ←→, drag to change the width of the Taskbar.

Moving the Taskbar is quite easy to do by mistake, so it is just as well to know how to do it intentionally – if only to correct a mistake!

Resizing the Taskbar – making it deeper, or wider – is sometimes useful. Narrow vertical displays are almost unreadable.

When you are running a lot of programs with a horizontal Taskbar, the titles on the buttons can be very small. If you deepen the display, you get two rows of decent-sized buttons.

Take note

If you like to keep the Taskbar visible, it takes least space at the top or bottom of the screen.

If you have a lot of applications running at once, or several toolbars on the Taskbar (see page 84), then the Taskbar is best at the left or right edge, but with Auto-Hide turned on.

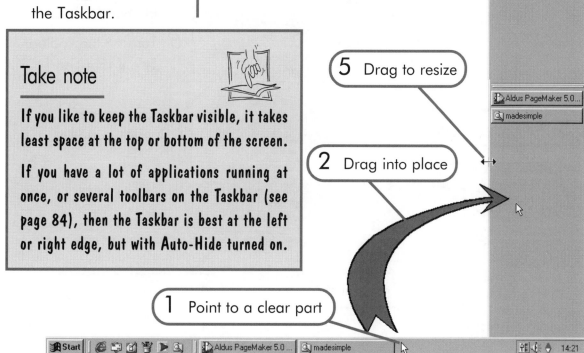

5 Drag to resize

2 Drag into place

1 Point to a clear part

Taskbar Toolbars

Basic steps

The normal setting for the Taskbar is to have the Quick Launch Toolbar, plus buttons for any open applications and the Clock.

If you find that you do not use it, Quick Launch can be removed, to allow more space for application buttons.

If you like working from the Taskbar, other Toolbars can be added, turning the Taskbar into the main starting point for all your commonly-used activities.

□ Adding Toolbars

1 Right-click on an empty place on the Taskbar to open its context menu.

2 Point to Toolbars.

3 Click on a Toolbar to add it to (or remove it from) the Taskbar.

□ Toolbar options

4 Right-click on a Taskbar Toolbar to open its context menu.

5 Point to View and set the button size.

6 Turn on the Toolbar Title if required.

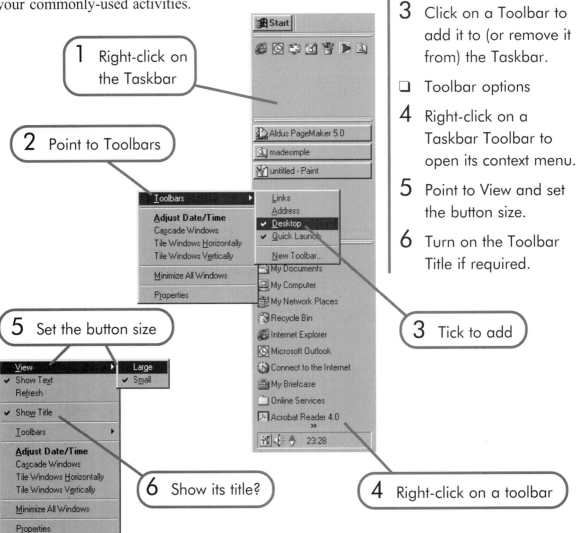

1 Right-click on the Taskbar

2 Point to Toolbars

5 Set the button size

6 Show its title?

3 Tick to add

4 Right-click on a toolbar

Basic steps

1 Create a new folder –
   it can be in any con-
   venient place.

2 Set up shortcuts to you
   main programs.

3 Open the Taskbar
   menu, point to
   Toolbars and select
   New Toolbar.

4 Select your new folder.

5 Click [OK].

Tip

**If you add toolbars to the
Taskbar, a horizontal display will get too crowded
to see things properly unless you have it more than
one line deep (see the
example below). Other-
wise, drag it to a side
position, make it wide
enough for the buttons to
fit and turn on AutoHide.**

Creating a new toolbar

If you like the Taskbar as a means of starting programs, you can
set up new Taskbar Toolbars to hold your own collections of
shortcuts to programs that you use regularly.

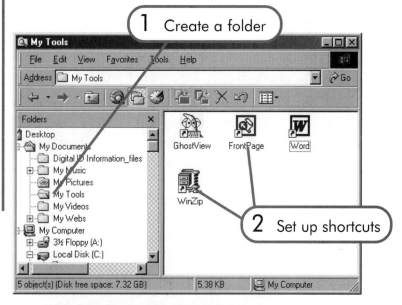

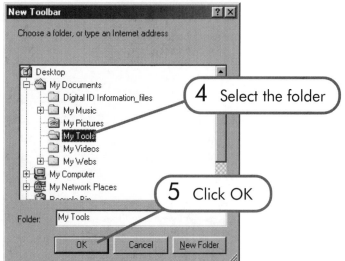

85

The Start menu

When Windows Me was installed on your system, it created a Start menu that included shortcuts to all its own applications and accessories. If you had upgraded from Windows 98, it will have included all the entries in the old Start menu. When you install new software on your system, the installation routine should also bring them into the Start menu.

If it gets built automatically, why would we want to mess around with it? The answer is that installation routines can only do so much. They may not structure the menus as you would like, and you will sometimes come across software – particulary shareware – that does not install itself into the Windows menus.

The Advanced panel of the Taskbar and Start Menu Properties box gives you control of your menu structure.

Take note

The Start menu is a folder in the Windows folder. Its submenus are subfolders and the entries are short- cuts in those folders. You can manage your Start menu by adding, deleting or moving files and fold- ers through Windows Explorer – but it's easier to start from the buttons on the Properties panel.

Use these buttons to change the entries on your menus

'Expanding' a folder adds its contents as a submenu

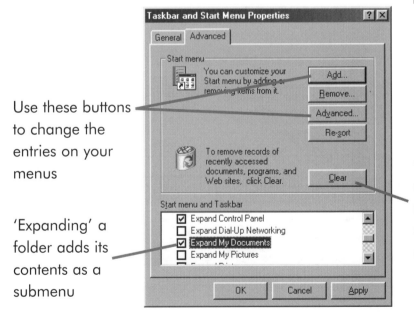

Click to empty the Documents list in the Start menu – though there's not usually much point, as newer ones constantly replace the older entries.

Basic steps

1 Open the Taskbar & Start Menu dialog box.

2 Click [Add...].

3 Click [Browse...] and find and select the program.

4 Select the menu folder to hold the new entry.

5 Replace the program's filename with a more meaningful name.

You can add individually, any programs that were not handled by the installation routines. All that is essential is that you know where to find them.

You can type the path and filename if you know it

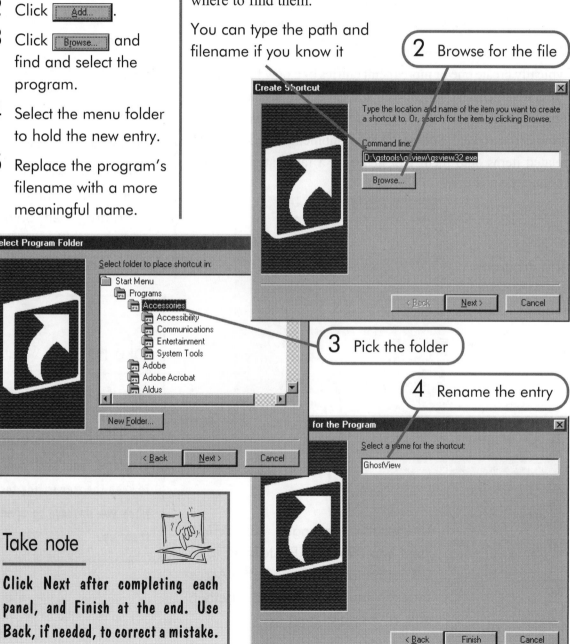

2 Browse for the file

3 Pick the folder

4 Rename the entry

Take note

Click Next after completing each panel, and Finish at the end. Use Back, if needed, to correct a mistake.

Organising the menu

The Advanced button takes you into Windows Explorer, with the focus on the Start menu folder. Here you can reorganise, rename, delete and create shortcuts and move them into menu folders. The job you are most likely to want to do is reorganise.

When you run the installion routine for new software, it will typically create one or more menu entries or a new folder in the Programs menu. This is all well and good, but after a while the Programs menu can get huge – I've seen them wrap twice around the screen! Setting up new submenus, and grouping related items onto them will give you a far neater and more usable menu system.

❏ Making a submenu

1 Click Advanced... .

2 Select the Programs folder.

3 Open the File menu and select New – Folder.

4 Rename the folder.

5 Select the relevant folders and entries and drag them onto the new folder.

6 Close Explorer.

This Programs menu is getting too crowded!

The graphics packages – QuickTime, Paint Shop Pro and PhotoStyler (plus GIF animator and Paint in the Accessories) – could be grouped together onto a Graphics menu.

Take note

Even if you use the personalised Start menu, which hides little-used programs, you still need to keep the menus tidy for when you do have to open them up.

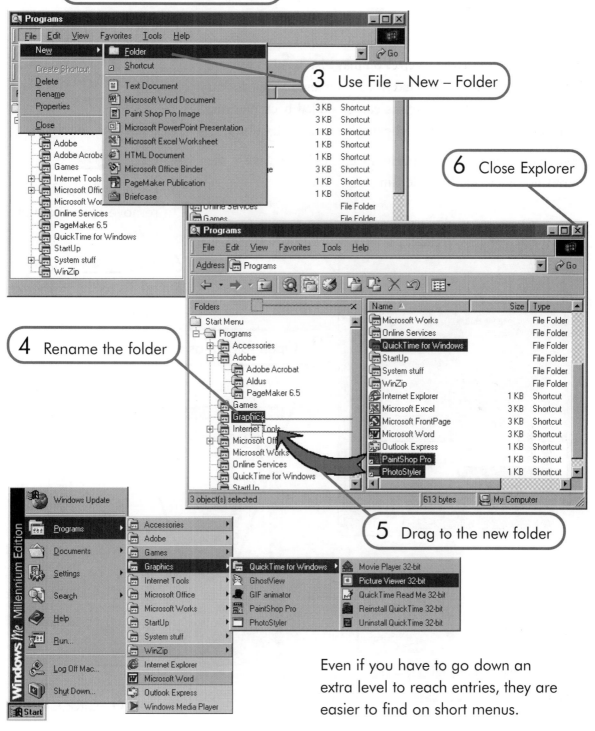

2 Select the Programs folder

3 Use File – New – Folder

6 Close Explorer

4 Rename the folder

5 Drag to the new folder

Even if you have to go down an extra level to reach entries, they are easier to find on short menus.

Removing entries

If you remove software from your system, you may also need to remove its entry from the Start menu – uninstall programs don't always do a clean sweep. You may also want to remove some of the entries that Windows Me created when it was installed. If necessary, programs can be added back onto the menu later, or run by double-clicking on them in Explorer.

Don't worry too much about deleting entries by mistake – the entries go first to the Recycle Bin.

1 Click [Remove...].

2 Open up sub-folders if necessary, until you can see the entry.

3 Select the entry.

4 Click [Remove].

5 Repeat Steps 2 to 4 remove all unwanted entries.

6 Click [Close] to return to the Properties panel.

Taskbar and Start Menu Properties

General | Advanced

Start menu

You can customize your Start menu by adding or removing items from it.

[Add...]
[Remove...]
[Advanced...]
[Re-sort]

To remove records of recently accessed documents, programs, and Web sites, click Clear.

[Clear]

Start menu and Taskbar

☑ Expand Control Panel
☐ Expand Dial-Up Networking
☑ Expand My Documents
☐ Expand My Pictures

[OK] [Cancel] [Apply]

1 Click Remove...

2 Open folders as necessary

3 Select the entry

Remove Shortcuts/Folders

To remove an item from the Start menu, select the item and click Remove.

📁 Start Menu
  📁 Programs
    📁 Accessories
    📁 Adobe
    📁 Games
    📁 Graphics
    📁 Internet Tools
      📁 Internet Explorer
      📁 Online Services
        America Online
        Earthlink Internet Services
        Prodigy Internet
    📁 Real
    📁 Utilities

[Remove] [Close]

4 Click Remove

6 Click Close

Take note

You can remove whole folders – and their entries – if you need to.

90

Setting the Clock

1 Right-click on the Taskbar to open its context menu.

2 Select Adjust Date/Time.

3 Check the Time zone, and if necessary select the correct one from the drop-down list.

4 Pick the Month from the drop-down list.

5 Click on the Day.

6 Click on Hour, Minute or Second to select then either adjust with the arrows or type the correct value.

7 Click Apply to restart the clock.

We can't leave the Taskbar without having a look at adjusting the Date and Time. This should not need doing often – PCs keep good time, and Windows Me even puts the clock forward and back for Summer Time!

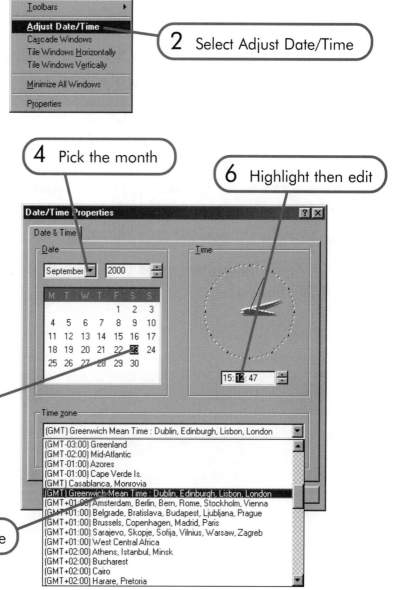

2 Select Adjust Date/Time

4 Pick the month

6 Highlight then edit

5 Set the day

3 Set the Time zone

Summary

❑ The Taskbar can be reduced to a thin line or allowed to lie behind active windows, but is easiest to use if it is visible and always on top.

❑ The Taskbar can be moved to any edge of the screen, and resized if needed.

❑ Toolbars on the Taskbar offer you another way to start programs. You can create your own Toolbars.

❑ The Start menu is a folder in the Windows folder. Its entries are folders or shortcuts to programs.

❑ You can add new entries to the menu by creating shortcuts and storing them in a chosen folder.

❑ The menu can be reorganised by moving entries to new or other existing folders.

❑ Unwanted menu entries are easily removed.

❑ The Clock can be adjusted in the Date/Time Properties dialog box.

7 The Control Panel

The settings

The **Control Panel** allows you to customise many of the features of Windows to your own need and tastes.

Some settings are best left at the defaults defined by Windows; some should be set when new hardware or software is added to the system; some should be set once then left alone; a few can be fiddled with whenever you feel like a change.

Some of the key control settings that can or should be adjusted are covered in this section.

Basic steps

1 Click 🄰Start and point to Settings then select Control Panel.

2 If you are in Web mode, click on <u>view all Control Panel options</u>.

3 Double-click an icon to change its settings.

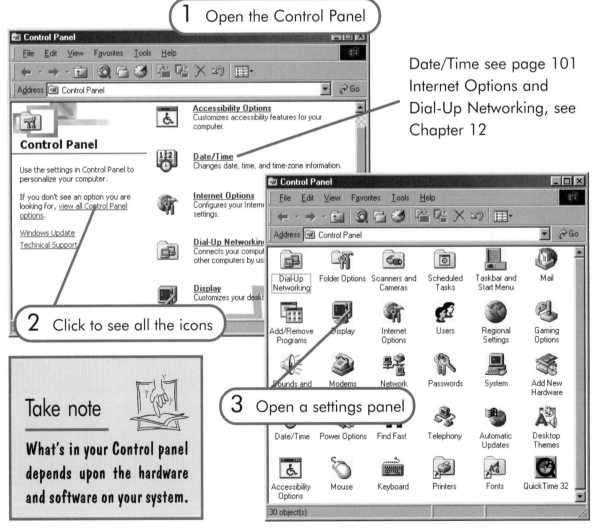

1 Open the Control Panel

Date/Time see page 101
Internet Options and Dial-Up Networking, see Chapter 12

2 Click to see all the icons

3 Open a settings panel

Take note

What's in your Control panel depends upon the hardware and software on your system.

Display

The Display

This may seem to be pure frills and fancies, but it does have a serious purpose. If you spend a lot of time in front of your screen, being able to see it clearly and use it comfortably is important.

Background panel

The **Wallpaper** is the background to the desktop. Some are hideous, but others are acceptable. The supplied designs can be edited with Paint, if you feel artistic, or you can use any graphic (preferably BMP or JPG) of your own. With a large image, set it in the **Centre** rather than duplicate it as a **Tile**.

If you prefer a single colour background, you may want to impose a **Pattern** on it.

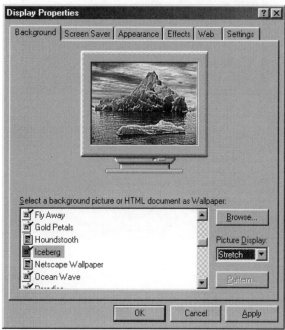

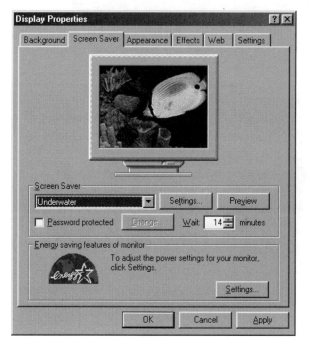

Screen Savers

These are fun but serve little real purpose nowadays. (On an old monitor, if a static image was left on too long, it could burn into the screen.) A screen saver switches to a moving image after the system has been left inactive for a few minutes. **Preview** the ones that are on offer. **Settings** allows you to adjust the images.

There is a small industry churning out weird and wonderful screen savers for you to buy, if you want something different.

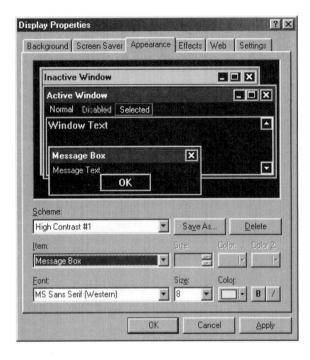

Appearance

This controls the colour schemes and the size of fonts. There is a set of ready-made schemes, or you can select individual parts of the screen from the **Item** list and adjust the **Colour** or **Font**. The scheme can then be saved with a new name.

There are **High Contrast** and coloured **Large** and **Extra large** (font) schemes if easy viewing is needed.

If you make a mess of the scheme – easily done! – restore the appearance by selecting the **Windows Standard**.

Effects

Don't like the standard Desktop icons? Here's your chance to change them. You can pick from a large set of alternatives, or use icons that you have created or found on the Internet. If you are treating the screen as a Web page, the icons may get in the way and can be turned off.

The Visual Effects are mainly cosmetic. Large icons are useful as part of a high visibility scheme. The remaining options produce a slicker, smoother display, though they make the system work a little harder.

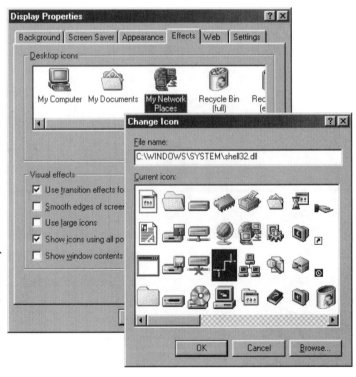

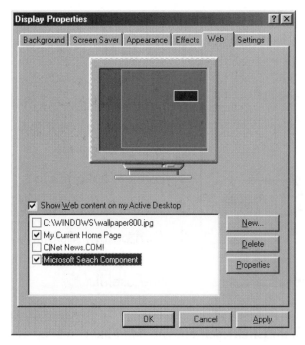

Web

This panel controls the key **Active Desktop** settings. If you do not want the integration with the Internet, turn off the **Show Web content on my Active Desktop** option. Otherwise, start here to add elements to your Desktop. Click **New…** when you are online, to go to Microsoft to see what's on offer. The selection is not huge, but you may find some of them useful – for example, the *Search Component* offers a convenient way to start an Internet search.

You can also reach this panel by right-clicking on the Desktop and selecting **Active Desktop – Customize my Desktop** from the menu.

Settings

Play with the other panels as much as you like, but treat this one with respect. In particular, leave the **Advanced** options alone unless you are unhappy with the current display *and* know what you are doing. You can switch to a display mode that it not properly supported by your hardware, resulting in a screen which is difficult or impossible to read – and therefore to correct!

If you do produce an unreadable screen, reboot the system using the Startup disk – you did make one, didn't you – and restore the default setting from there.

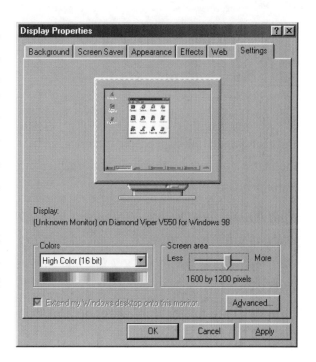

Adjusting the mouse

Mouse

Don't change to **Left-handed** unless you are the only one who uses the system, and it is the only system that you use. You will only confuse yourself and others.

The **Double-Click Speed** determines the difference between a proper double click and two separate clicks.

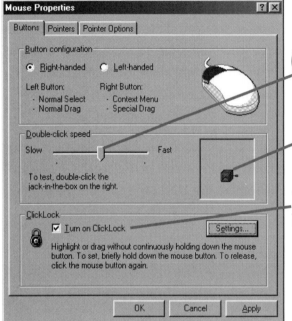

- Buttons tab
1 Set the Double-click speed.
2 Double-click in the Test area to see if the system responds.
- Pointer Options tab
3 Set the Pointer Speed.
4 Turn on any Visibility options that you might find useful.

With **ClickLock** on, you don't have to keep the button down when dragging an object on screen

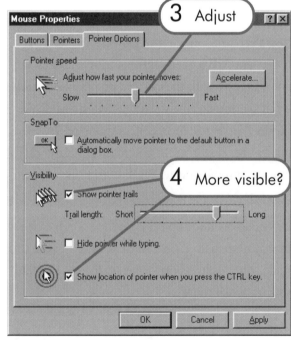

Pointer Speed links speed and distance, so that the faster you move the mouse, the further the pointer goes.

*Find Pointer and Double-click speeds that suit you and **stick with them**. If you keep fiddling with these, you will never get the feel of the mouse.*

Pointer Trails make the mouse easier to see on the LCD screens of portables.

Basic steps

Pointers

- ❏ Pointers tab
- 1 Pick a Scheme.
- 2 Select an action.
- 3 Click [Browse...].
- 4 Pick a cursor image for the action.
- 5 Click [Open].
- 6 Repeat Steps 2 to 5 for any other actions.
- 7 Click [OK].

There are alternative Schemes, including ones with large and extra large pointers. You can also pick your own images (and animated ones from any Desktop themes you have installed) to link to chosen mouse actions.

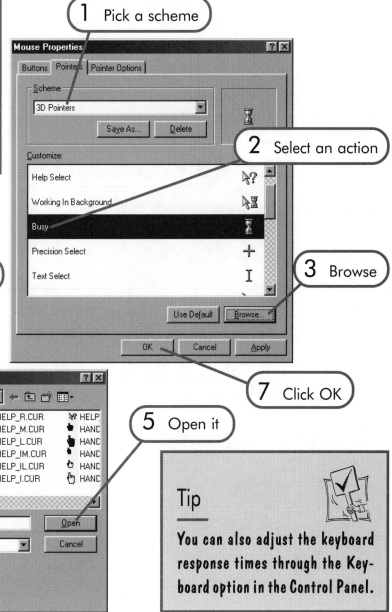

Check out
the Preview

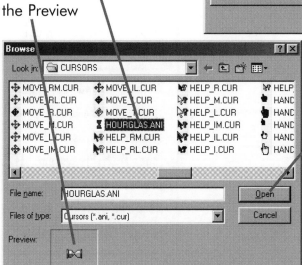

Tip

You can also adjust the keyboard response times through the Keyboard option in the Control Panel.

Sounds

Sounds

Windows allows you to attach sounds to events. These can be seen as useful ways of alerting you to what's happening or as more modern noise pollution. It all depends upon your point of view. I like a fanfare when the system is ready to start work (to wake me up – well, you wait so long!) but few other sounds. Try them out – the Utopia sounds are worth listening to.

The other tabs can be used to change the Audio and Voice devices or fine-tune their volume controls. The devices are best left to the system. The volume controls can be reached more simply from the 📢 icon on the Taskbar.

Basic steps

1 Pick a Scheme

2 Select an event.

3 Click ▶ to Preview its sound.

4 Sample a few more.

5 Go back to Step 1 and try alternative schemes until you have found the one you like best.

6 To set individual sounds, Browse for an alternative, or select [none] for the Name.

7 Click Apply or OK .

2 Select an event

3 Preview its sound

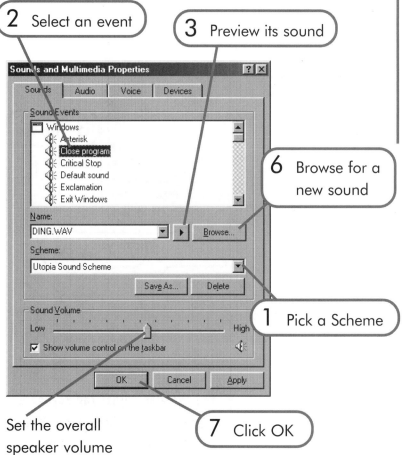

6 Browse for a new sound

1 Pick a Scheme

Set the overall speaker volume

7 Click OK

Take note

With a sound card and speakers, the quality of sound compares well to a (cheap) HiFi system. If you are limited to the PC's own speaker, you do not get the same quality!

Basic steps

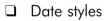

Regional
Settings

Regional settings

❏ Date styles

1 Run Regional Settings.

2 Open the Date tab.

3 Set the range for the two-digit date.

4 Pick a Short date style from the list and edit it to your taste.

5 Click ⬚Apply⬚.

6 Repeat steps 4 and 5 for the Long date.

7 Point to the Taskbar clock and see how it looks.

These control the units of measurement and the styles used by most applications for displaying dates, time, currency and other numbers. The choice of Region in the top tab sets the defaults. The other tabs are for fine-tuning the styles. The **Date** tab is a good example. In the **Calendar** section you can tell the system how to interpret two-digit dates – when you say '50' do you mean '1950' or '2050'? In the **Short date** and **Long date** sections you can select and define their display style. Both use the same coding:

Day	Month	
d	M	Number
dd	MM	Number with leading 0 if needed
ddd	MMM	Three-letter name
dddd	MMMM	Full name
Year	yy for 01; yyyy for 2001	

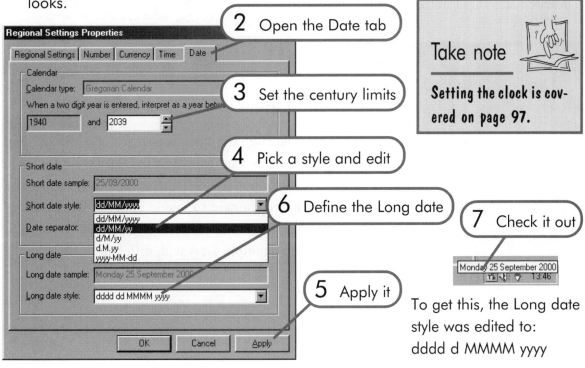

2 Open the Date tab

3 Set the century limits

4 Pick a style and edit

6 Define the Long date

5 Apply it

7 Check it out

Take note

Setting the clock is covered on page 97.

To get this, the Long date style was edited to:
dddd d MMMM yyyy

Accessibility

Accessibility
Options

These offer a range of ways to make life easier for people with sight, hearing or motor control disabilities – though the keyboard alternative to the mouse may well be useful to other people as well.

Keyboard

With **StickyKeys** you can type [Ctrl], [Shift] and [Alt] combinations by pressing one key at a time, rather than all at once.

FilterKeys solves the problem of repetition of keystrokes caused by slow typing.

ToggleKeys play sounds when any of the Lock keys are pressed.

Sound

These replace sound warnings with visible alerts.

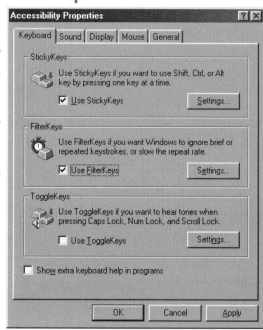

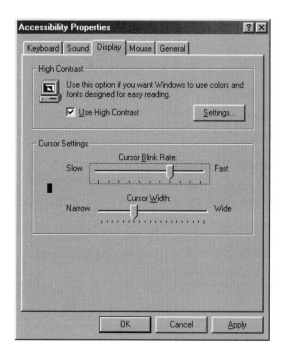

Display

The High Contrast displays can be selected from here, as well as from the Display panel. If you click the Settings... button, you can set up a keyboard shortcut to toggle between High Contrast and normal displays – very useful if the computer has multiple users with different needs.

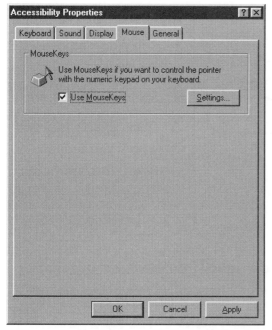

Mouse

With this turned on, the arrow keys on the Number pad can be used to move the mouse, and the central [5] acts as the left mouse button. It is more limited than the mouse – you can only move up, down, left or right and not diagonally – but it is easier to control.

Click the **Settings...** button to open the Settings for MouseKeys dialog box, where you can experiment to find the most workable levels.

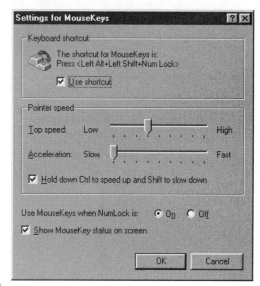

General

If you are using any of the Accessibility options, check this panel to make sure that they are turning on and off as and when you want them.

This illustration shows the standard High Contrast display setting. If required, larger fonts could be set for the panel and button text.

Add/Remove Programs  Basic steps

Any software written to the Windows standards should be easy to install and – just as important – easy to remove. Unwanted parts of the Windows Me can also be removed – and you can add accessories that were omitted during the initial installation.

☐ Removing Programs

1 Run Add/Remove Programs.

2 Select the program.

3 Click [Add/Remove..] and wait – you may be asked to confirm the removal of some files – if in doubt, keep them.

> 1 Go to Add/Remove Programs

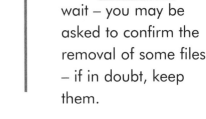

You can install from here, but it is simpler to use any new software's Setup routine

> 2 Select the program

> 3 Click Add/Remove

Some files may be left – check through Explorer

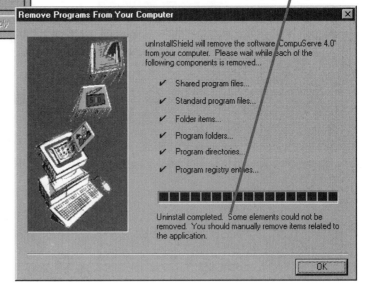

Take note

You may need the original disks or CD-ROM to uninstall some software.

❏ Trimming Windows

4 Go to Windows Setup and wait while it checks your system.

5 To remove an entire set of related files, click on the checkbox to clear it.

6 To remove individual files from a set, select the set and click
Details... .

7 Clear the checkboxes for unwanted items then click OK .

8 At the main panel, click OK to start the removals.

Take note

To add new accessories or other features, tick the checkboxes instead of clearing them!

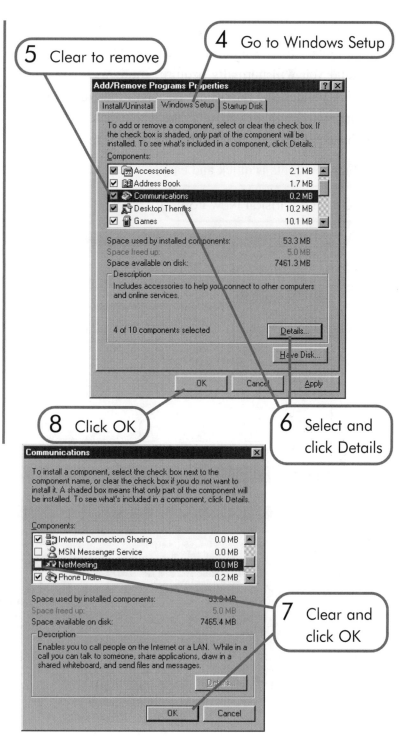

5 Clear to remove

4 Go to Windows Setup

Add/Remove Programs Properties

Install/Uninstall | Windows Setup | Startup Disk |

To add or remove a component, select or clear the check box. If the check box is shaded, only part of the component will be installed. To see what's included in a component, click Details.

Components:

☑ 🖼 Accessories   2.1 MB
☑ 📧 Address Book   1.7 MB
☑ 🌐 Communications   0.2 MB
☑ 🖼 Desktop Themes   10.2 MB
☑ 🎮 Games   10.1 MB

Space used by installed components: 53.3 MB
Space freed up: 5.0 MB
Space available on disk: 7461.3 MB

Description
Includes accessories to help you connect to other computers and online services.

4 of 10 components selected   Details...

Have Disk...

OK   Cancel   Apply

8 Click OK

6 Select and click Details

Communications

To install a component, select the check box next to the component name, or clear the check box if you do not want to install it. A shaded box means that only part of the component will be installed. To see what's included in a component, click Details.

Components:

☑ 📡 Internet Connection Sharing   0.0 MB
☐ 👤 MSN Messenger Service   0.0 MB
☐ 📞 NetMeeting   0.0 MB
☑ 📞 Phone Dialer   0.2 MB

Space used by installed components: 53.3 MB
Space freed up: 5.0 MB
Space available on disk: 7465.4 MB

Description
Enables you to call people on the Internet or a LAN. While in a call you can talk to someone, share applications, draw in a shared whiteboard, and send files and messages.

Details...

7 Clear and click OK

OK   Cancel

Fonts

Fonts

There is one school of thought that says you can never have enough fonts. There is a decent core supplied with Windows itself, and you will normally acquire more with any word-processor and desktop publishing packages that you install. If these are not enough for you, there are whole disks full of fonts available commercially and through the shareware distributors.

Installing new fonts is quick and easy.

❑ Adding fonts

1 Place the disk of new fonts into a drive.

2 Open the File menu and select Install New Font.

3 Select the drive and folder and wait while the system reads the names of the fonts on the disk.

4 Click [Select All], or work through the list and select the ones you want to install.

5 Click [OK].

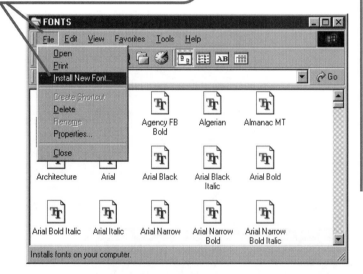

2 Use File – Install New Font

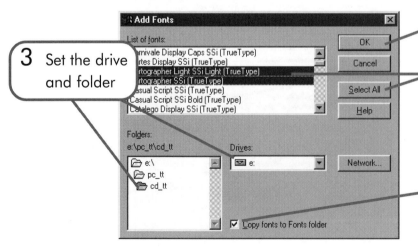

5 Click OK

3 Set the drive and folder

4 Select All or some

If the fonts are already in a folder on a hard drive, you don't need to copy the files

Basic steps

1 Click AB the Similarity tool.

2 Pick a font to list by, then select and Open it from its context menu.

3 Select and Open any *Very Similar* font.

4 Click [Done] to close the viewer.

5 If it is not useful, press [Delete] to remove it.

Removing unwanted fonts

This will save space on the hard disk, speed up Windows' Start Up and produce a shorter set to hunt through when you are setting a font in an application. Listing fonts by similarity helps to identify unnecessary ones.

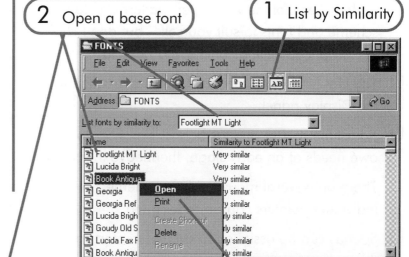

2 Open a base font

1 List by Similarity

4 Click Done

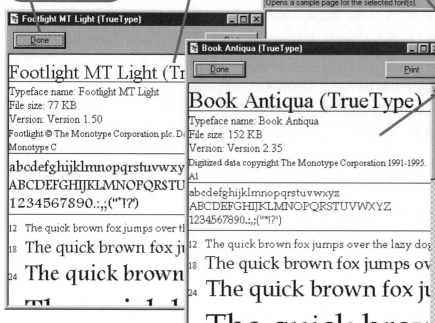

3 Open a Very Similar font

There can be subtle differences between the screen and printed appearance of a font – print a sample for a closer look.

Summary

❑ The Control Panel contains routines that determine the settings of some of the most basic features of how Windows works.

❑ The Display give you plenty of scope for personal preferences. Set the wallpaper, patterns, colour scheme and fonts to suit yourself – but don't change the Advanced Settings unless you have to.

❑ The key Active Desktop settings are controlled from the Display panel.

❑ Adjust the mouse and keyboard responses to your own needs at an early stage, then leave them alone.

❑ There are several mouse pointer schemes, and individual pointers can be redesigned.

❑ Sounds can be assigned to events, to alert you when things happen.

❑ The Regional settings control the appearance of dates, times, currency and numbers in most Windows Applications.

❑ Windows Me has a number of Accessibility Options to make the screen easier to read and the mouse and keyboard easier to control.

❑ To delete unwanted software, or parts of the Windows Me setup, use Add/Remove Programs.

❑ New Fonts can be installed easily. It is just as easy to examine fonts and to remove unnecessary ones.

8 Printers

Printer settings

Windows Me knows about printers, just as it knows about most other bits of hardware that you might attach to your system. If you installed Me over an earlier version of Windows, it will have picked up the printer settings from there. If yours was a new Windows Me computer and you have just installed a printer (see page 112), check the settings now. Make sure that they are how you would normally want to use the printer – the settings can be changed for any special print job, using the Print Setup routine of any application program.

Basic steps

1 Click **Start**.

2 Point to Settings.

3 Select Printers.

4 Right-click a printer to open its short menu.

5 Select Properties. Work through the panels, selecting settings to suit your normal print needs.

2 Point to Settings

3 Select Printers

1 Click Start

Take note

Different types of printers have different types of properties. Some of the examples given here may not apply to your machine.

Tip

The fax is also a 'printer'. Paper size, greyscales and other 'printing' aspects are controlled from here.

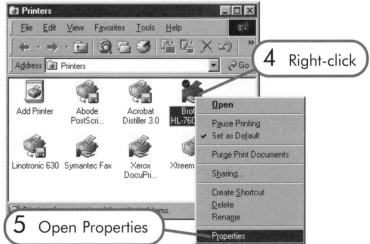

4 Right-click

5 Open Properties

All printers have a Paper tab, with Paper Size and Orientation options. Alternative Layouts are normally only found on Postscript printers

If your printer can work at different resolutions, remember that the higher the resolution, the slower the printing – and the more ink/toner it uses.

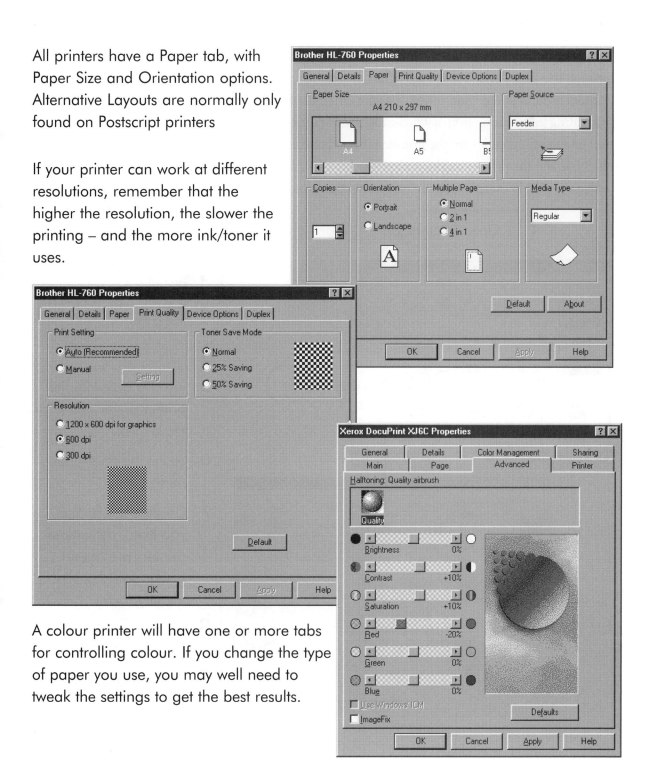

A colour printer will have one or more tabs for controlling colour. If you change the type of paper you use, you may well need to tweak the settings to get the best results.

Adding a printer

Adding a new printer is simple. There is a wizard to take you through the steps, and Windows Me has drivers for almost all printers around at the time of its design. (Drivers convert the formatting information from a word-processor or other application into the right codes for the printer.) If you have a *very* new machine, use the drivers on the printer's setup disk, otherwise, you are probably better using the drivers on the Windows CD.

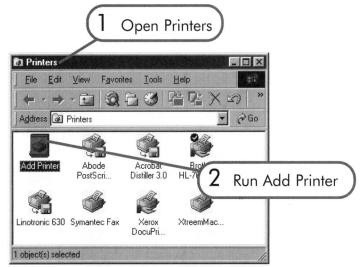

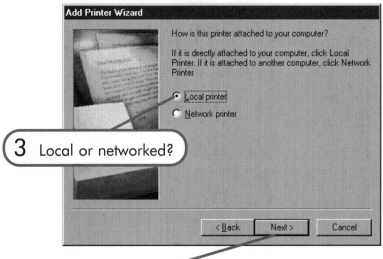

Click Next after completing each step

1 Open the Printers folder.

2 Run Add Printer to start the Wizard.

3 If you are on a network, select Local (attached to your PC) or Network printer.

Either

4 Pick the Manufacturer then the Printer from the lists.

or

5 Insert a disk with the printer driver and click Have Disk.

6 Select the Port – normally LPT1.

7 Change the name if you like – networked printers are often given nicknames to identify them.

8 Set this as the default if appropriate.

9 At the final stage opt for the test print then click Finish and wait.

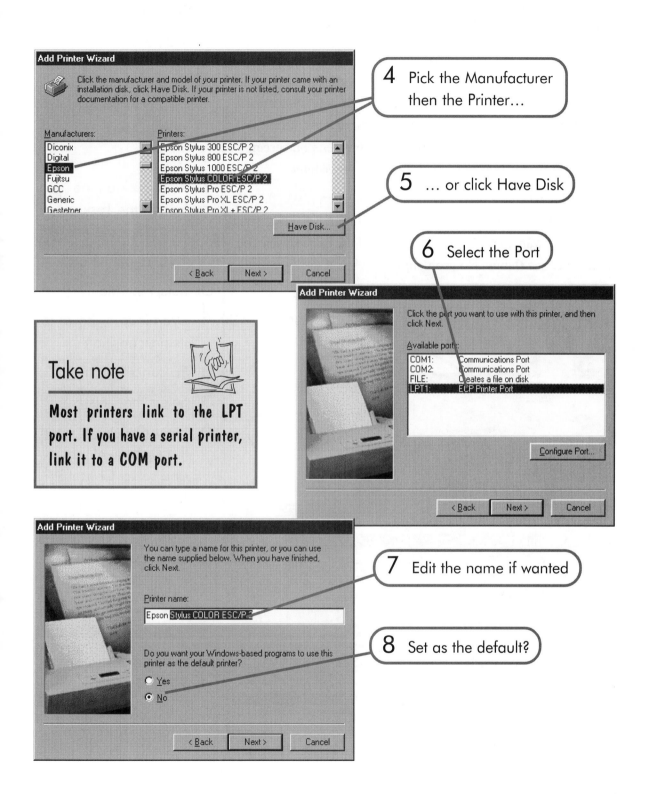

Add Printer Wizard

Click the manufacturer and model of your printer. If your printer came with an installation disk, click Have Disk. If your printer is not listed, consult your printer documentation for a compatible printer.

Manufacturers:
- Diconix
- Digital
- Epson
- Fujitsu
- GCC
- Generic
- Gestetner

Printers:
- Epson Stylus 300 ESC/P 2
- Epson Stylus 800 ESC/P 2
- Epson Stylus 1000 ESC/P 2
- Epson Stylus COLOR ESC/P 2
- Epson Stylus Pro ESC/P 2
- Epson Stylus Pro XL ESC/P 2
- Epson Stylus Pro XL + ESC/P 2

Have Disk...

< Back   Next >   Cancel

4 Pick the Manufacturer then the Printer...

5 ... or click Have Disk

6 Select the Port

Add Printer Wizard

Click the port you want to use with this printer, and then click Next.

Available ports:

COM1:	Communications Port
COM2:	Communications Port
FILE:	Creates a file on disk
LPT1:	ECP Printer Port

Configure Port...

< Back   Next >   Cancel

Take note

Most printers link to the LPT port. If you have a serial printer, link it to a COM port.

Add Printer Wizard

You can type a name for this printer, or you can use the name supplied below. When you have finished, click Next.

Printer name:

Epson Stylus COLOR ESC/P 2

Do you want your Windows-based programs to use this printer as the default printer?

- ○ Yes
- ● No

< Back   Next >   Cancel

7 Edit the name if wanted

8 Set as the default?

Managing the queue

When you send a document for printing, Windows Me will happily handle it in the background. It prepares the file for the printer, stores it in a queue if the printer is already busy or off-line, pushes the pages out one at a time and deletes the temporary files it has created. Nothing visible happens on screen – unless the printer runs out of paper or has other faults.

This is fine when things run smoothly. However, if you decide you want to cancel the printing of a document, or have sent several and want to push one to the head of the queue, then you do need to see things. No problem!

1 Open the Printers folder, right-click on the active printer and select Open.

Or

2 Right-click on the 🖨 icon in the Taskbar and select the printer.

❑ To change the order

3 Select the file.

4 Drag it up or down to its new position.

❑ To cancel printing

5 Select the file(s).

6 Press [Delete] or open the Document menu and select Cancel Printing.

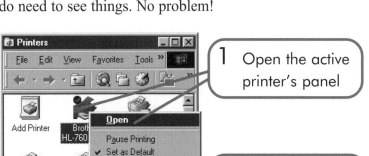

1 Open the active printer's panel

2 Select the printer

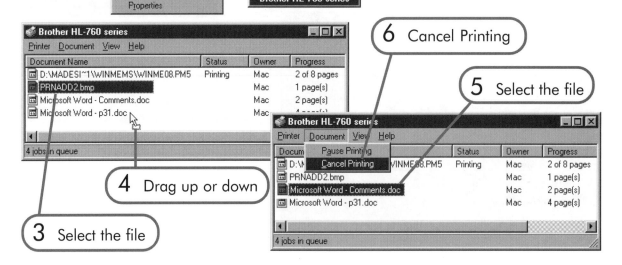

6 Cancel Printing

5 Select the file

4 Drag up or down

3 Select the file

114

Direct printing

1 Open the Printers folder or the one for the target printer.

2 Open the folder containing the document file to be printed.

3 Arrange the windows so that you can see both clearly.

4 Drag and drop the file on the printer icon (or into the target printer's folder).

❑ Windows will open the related application, print from there then close the application.

You do not necessarily have to load a document into an application to print it. Windows Me can print many types of documents directly from the files.

Bitmapped graphics (.BMP files), plain text and the documents from any Microsoft Office application can be printed in this way, as can those from other newer software.

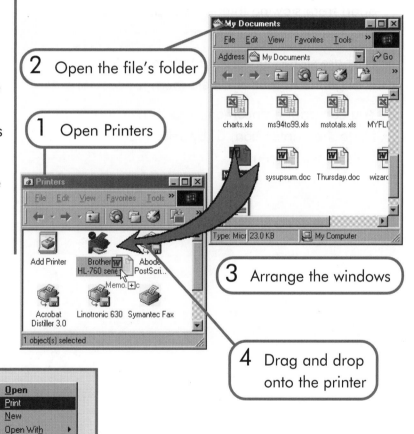

2 Open the file's folder

1 Open Printers

3 Arrange the windows

4 Drag and drop onto the printer

Tip

You can also print a file by right-clicking on it and selecting Print from the context menu.

115

Summary

❑ Printer settings can be adjusted if wanted. The Paper and resolution options should be checked.

❑ Adding a new printer is easy. Windows Me has drivers for almost all printers, though you may need a manufacturer's disk with very new models.

❑ Printing is handled in the background, so that – apart from slowing things up a bit – it does not interfere with your other work.

❑ Files are stored in a queue before printing. You can change their order or delete them if necessary.

❑ You can print a document directly by dragging the file to the printer icon, or by selecting Print from the file's context menu.

9 Disk housekeeping

The System Tools

These programs will help to keep your disks in good condition, and your data safe.

Disk Cleanup – finds and removes unused files;

Disk Defragmenter – optimises the organisation of storage to maximize the disk's speed and efficiency;

DriveSpace – can be used to create more storage space on floppy disks, or on older, smaller hard drives;

Maintenance Wizard – runs Disk Cleanup, ScanDisk and Disk Defragmenter. Can be set to run automatically.

NetWatcher – is used for monitoring activity on a network (see Chapter 10).

Scandisk – finds and fixes errors in data stored on disks;

Scheduled Tasks – lets you perform maintenance at set times;

System Information – gives (technical) information about what's going on inside your computer;

System Restore – backs up essential files, so that the system can be restored to normal after a crash.

Basic steps

1 Click ⚑Start.

2 Point to Programs

3 Point to Accessories.

4 Point to System Tools.

5 Click to select a tool.

Character Map and Clipboard Viewer are accessories, not tools – I don't know why Windows Me puts them on this menu.

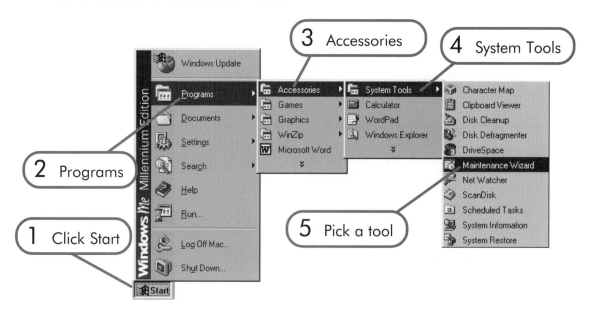

Basic steps

1 Open My Computer, right-click on the drive for the context menu.

2 Select Properties.

3 Bring the Tools tab to the front.

4 Select a tool.

Routine chores

The two system tools that are needed for the routine housekeeping can also be reached from the Properties box of any disk. The messages will remind you of chores you have been neglecting!

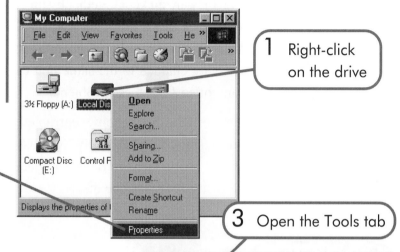

(1 Right-click on the drive)

(2 Select Properties)

(3 Open the Tools tab)

(4 Pick a tool)

This is Scandisk

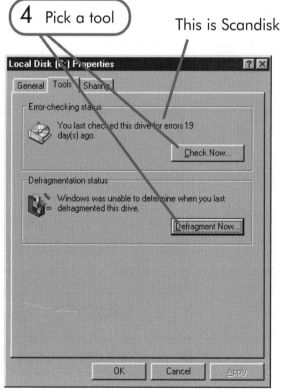

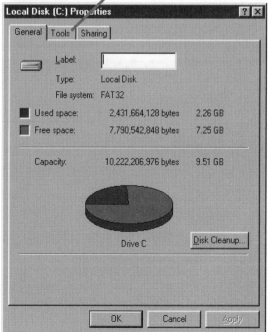

Use this panel to check how much space you have left on a disk.

Scandisk

Data is stored on disks in *allocation units*. A small file may fit on a single unit, but others are spread over many. A file's units may be in a continuous run or scattered over the disk (see *Disk Defragmenter,* page 124), but they are all kept together by links from one to the next. Sometimes these links get corrupted leaving *Lost fragments*, with no known links to any file, or *Cross-linked files*, where two are chained to the same unit of data. Scandisk can find – and often fix – these problems.

Sometimes the magnetic surface of the disk becomes corrupted, creating *Bad sectors* where data cannot be stored safely. Scandisk can identify these and, with a bit of luck, retrieve any data written there and transfer it to a safe part of the disk.

1 Run Scandisk from the Start menu or the disk's Properties box.

2 Select the Drive to be scanned.

3 Normally go for the quicker Standard scan, to fix file errors only. Do a Thorough scan to check for bad sectors on new disks and then every couple of months.

4 Set Advanced options as required – see opposite.

5 Click [Start].

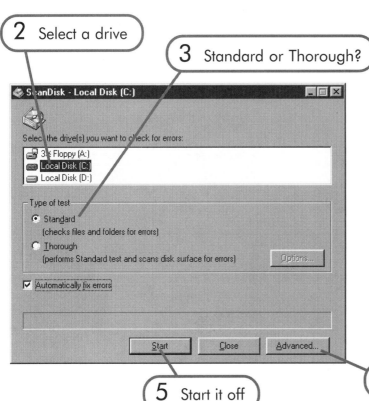

2 Select a drive

3 Standard or Thorough?

5 Start it off

4 Open the Advanced box

Take note

If the Standard scan finds bad sectors, it will offer to run a Thorough scan to fix them.

Advanced options

The *Summary* is always worth having.

The log records all that scandisk does – it can help to diagnose problems on a drive.

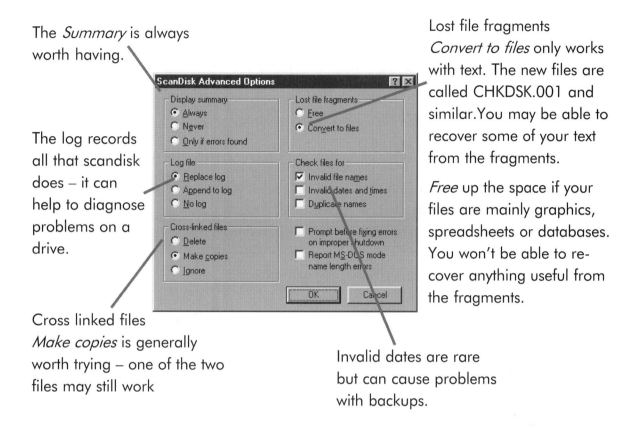

Lost file fragments *Convert to files* only works with text. The new files are called CHKDSK.001 and similar.You may be able to recover some of your text from the fragments.

Free up the space if your files are mainly graphics, spreadsheets or databases. You won't be able to re-cover anything useful from the fragments.

Cross linked files *Make copies* is generally worth trying – one of the two files may still work

Invalid dates are rare but can cause problems with backups.

Tip

If a floppy has any bad sectors on it, don't risk your data! Copy any files from the disk onto a good, new disk, and throw the dodgy one away.

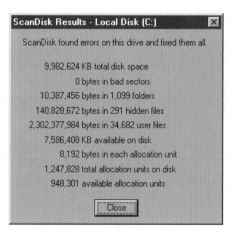

Scandisk has found some errors and fixed them. If it had found bad sectors, it would have helped to prevent future errors by mark-ing them off so that they could not be used.

Disk Defragmenter

Basic steps

When you first start to write data onto a disk, the files go on, one after the other, with each occupying a continuous run of disk space. When you access one of these files, the drive simply finds the start point, then reads the data in a single sweep.

After the disk has been in use for some time, holes begin to appear in the layout, and not all files are stored in a continuous area. Some have been deleted, others will have grown during editing, so that they no longer fit in their original slot, but now have parts stored elsewhere on the disk. When you store a new file, there may not be a single space large enough for it, and it is stored in scattered sections. The drive is becoming *fragmented*. The data is still safe, but the access speed will suffer as the drive now has to hunt for each fragment of the file.

Running Disk Defragmenter will pull scattered files together, so that they are stored in continuous blocks.

1. Run the Disk Defragmenter from the Start menu or the disk's Properties box.

2. Select the drive.

3. If you have run ScanDisk recently, click Settings... and turn off Check for errors.

4. Click OK.

5. When it starts, click Show Details to see what's going on.

6. Click Legend to find out what the symbols mean.

7. When it's finished, select another drive or click Exit.

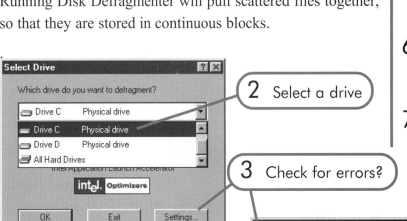

122

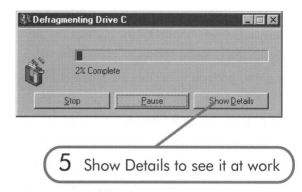

5 Show Details to see it at work

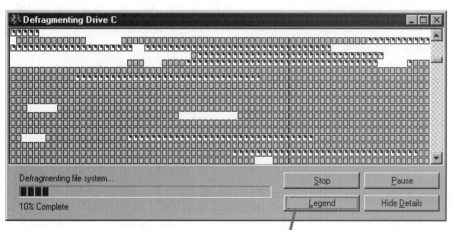

Watching Disk Defragmenter is more exciting than watching paint dry... but not much more

6 What does it all mean?

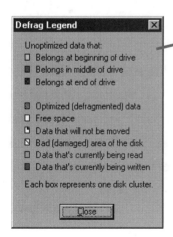

Disk Cleanup

This is a neat little utility, and well worth running regularly – especially if you spend much time on the Internet. When you are surfing the Net, your browser stores the files for the text, graphics and programs on the Web pages that you visit. This makes sense, as it means that if you go back to a page (either in the same session or at a later date), the browser can redraw it from the files, rather than having to download the whole lot again. However, if you don't revisit sites much, you can build up a lot of unwanted clutter on your disk. You can empty this cache from within your browser, but Cleanup will also do this.

The Recycle Bin can be emptied directly, or as part of the Cleanup.

Programs often create temporary files, but do not always remove them. Cleanup will also tidy up after them.

1 Run Disk Cleanup from the Start menu or click `Disk Cleanup...` on the disk's Properties panel.

2 After it has checked the system, the Cleanup panel opens. Select the areas to be cleaned.

3 Click `OK`.

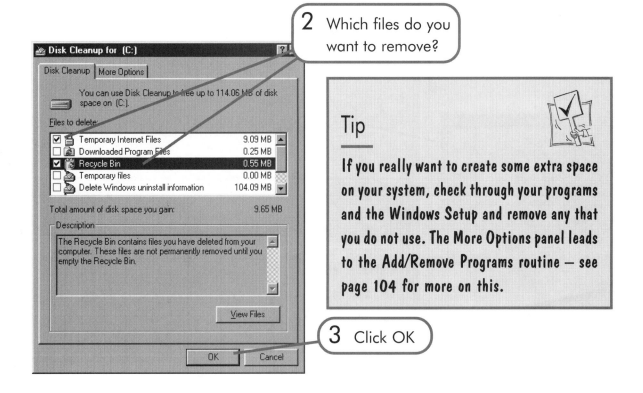

2 Which files do you want to remove?

Tip

If you really want to create some extra space on your system, check through your programs and the Windows Setup and remove any that you do not use. The More Options panel leads to the Add/Remove Programs routine – see page 104 for more on this.

3 Click OK

Basic steps

Maintenance Wizard

1 Run the Maintenance Wizard from the Start menu.

2 Select Perform maintenance now, click ❲ OK ❳ and leave it.

or

3 Select Change my maintenance settings or schedule, click ❲ OK ❳ and work through the Wizard.

4 Select Custom to set your own times.

5 Pick a time of day for the maintenance.

cont...

The Maintenance Wizard is a simple way to run the three most important housekeeping programs – Cleanup, Scandisk and Disk Defragmenter. It can be used two ways:

● Instant tune-up – just set it going and take a break from your machine while it works;

● Scheduled tasks – set it to run any or all of the chores at set, regular times.

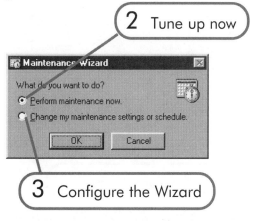

2 Tune up now

3 Configure the Wizard

4 Set your own schedules

5 Pick a time

6 Click Reschedule

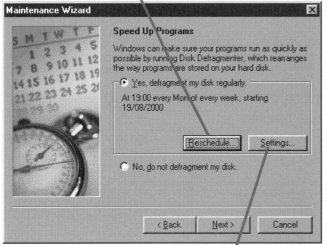

...cont

6 When you reach the Speed Up panel, click Reschedule...

7 Set the time, day and frequency for the task.

8 Click Settings...

9 Set the options for the program and click OK.

❑ Repeat Steps 7 and 8 for Scandisk and Disk Cleanup.

8 Click Settings

7 Set the day, time and frequency

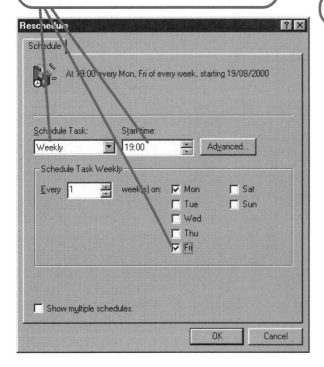

9 Set the program's options

Take note

The Settings for each program cover only the main options. For full control you must run the programs directly.

Basic steps

1 Select Scheduled Tasks from the System Tools menu.

2 Right-click on a task and select Properties.

3 To turn a task off, clear the Enabled box on the Task tab.

4 Use the Schedule tab to set new times.

5 Use the Settings tab to adjust how the task affects your work.

Scheduled Tasks

Running the Mainenance Wizard creates the set of Scheduled Tasks. You can run the Wizard again to change the schedules, but if you only want to adjust the settings of one task it is simpler to do it directly.

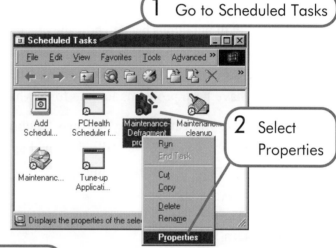

1 Go to Scheduled Tasks

2 Select Properties

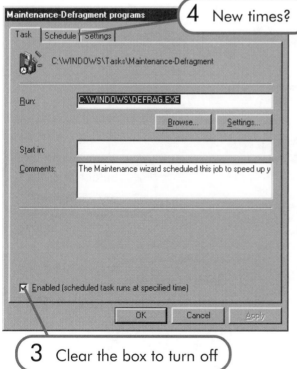

4 New times?

3 Clear the box to turn off

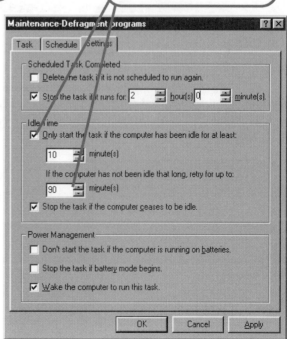

5 Adjust how it works

System Restore

You may never need to use this – but if you do, you will be very glad that it was there! System Restore helps you to recover from disaster. It works by taking copies of your essential files at regular intervals – once or twice a day. If any of those files become corrupted or erased – accidentally or otherwise – System Restore will put things back to how they were. Just run the application and select a restore point when things were well – normally the previous day's, but you may need to go back further if there have been problems lurking for a while.

For extra security, you can create your own 'restore points' before installing new software. A badly-designed application may occasionally mess up existing settings.

❑ Restore the system

1 Run System Restore.

2 Select Restore my computer to an earlier time and click ▐ Next ▌.

3 Pick a date and time and click ▐ Next ▌.

4 Confirm or cancel at the final screen.

❑ Create a restore point

5 Select Create a restore point and click ▐ Next ▌.

6 Enter a description and click ▐ Next ▌.

(1 Run System Restore)

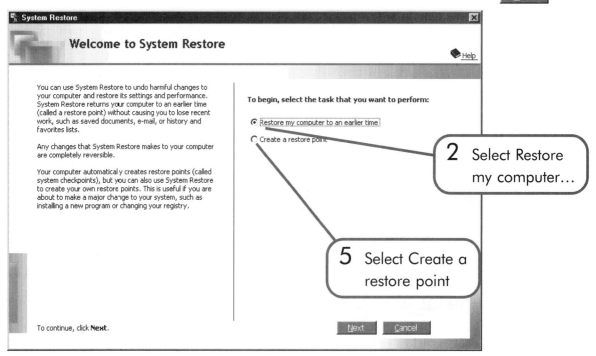

2 Select Restore my computer...

5 Select Create a restore point

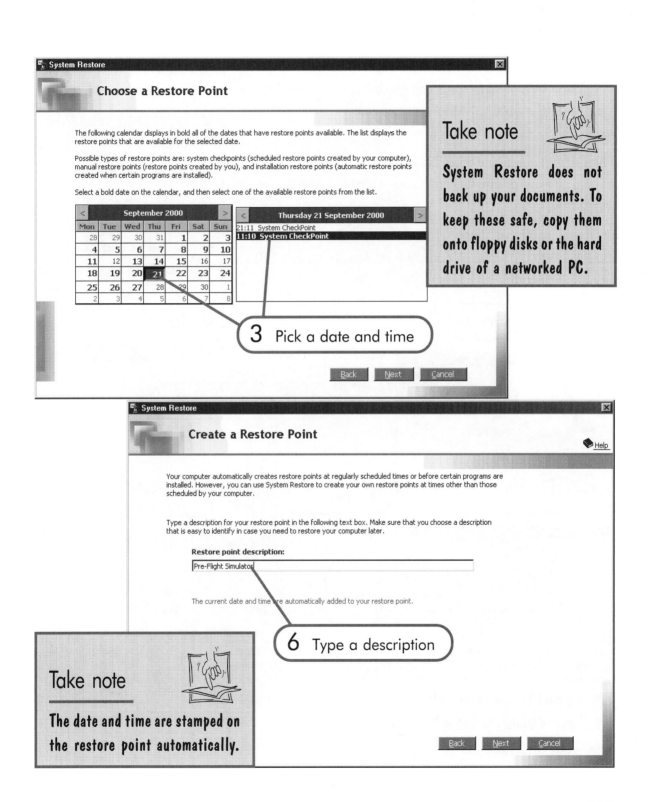

System Restore

Choose a Restore Point

The following calendar displays in bold all of the dates that have restore points available. The list displays the restore points that are available for the selected date.

Possible types of restore points are: system checkpoints (scheduled restore points created by your computer), manual restore points (restore points created by you), and installation restore points (automatic restore points created when certain programs are installed).

Select a bold date on the calendar, and then select one of the available restore points from the list.

<	September 2000					>
Mon	Tue	Wed	Thu	Fri	Sat	Sun
28	29	30	31	1	2	3
4	5	6	7	8	9	10
11	12	13	14	15	16	17
18	19	20	21	22	23	24
25	26	27	28	29	30	1
2	3	4	5	6	7	8

<	Thursday 21 September 2000	>
21:11 System CheckPoint
11:10 System CheckPoint

3 Pick a date and time

Back   Next   Cancel

Take note

System Restore does not back up your documents. To keep these safe, copy them onto floppy disks or the hard drive of a networked PC.

System Restore

Create a Restore Point

Help

Your computer automatically creates restore points at regularly scheduled times or before certain programs are installed. However, you can use System Restore to create your own restore points at times other than those scheduled by your computer.

Type a description for your restore point in the following text box. Make sure that you choose a description that is easy to identify in case you need to restore your computer later.

Restore point description:

Pre-Flight Simulator

The current date and time are automatically added to your restore point.

6 Type a description

Back   Next   Cancel

Take note

The date and time are stamped on the restore point automatically.

129

Formatting a floppy

Before you can use a new floppy disk, it must be **formatted**. This marks out magnetic tracks on the disk surface, dividing the area up into numbered blocks to provide organised storage space.

The **Format** command takes the hard work out of this – all you have to do is make sure that you know what kind of disk you are formatting.

PC disks are almost always High-Density (HD) standard – 3.5 inch, 1.44Mb capacities. You may occasionally meet a 720Kb Double-Density (DD) 3.5 inch disk.

Basic steps

1 Insert the disk into the drive.

2 Run My Computer or Explorer.

3 Right-click on the A: drive and select Format….

4 At the dialog box, make sure that it is set for the right capacity.

5 Select Full.

6 Click [Start].

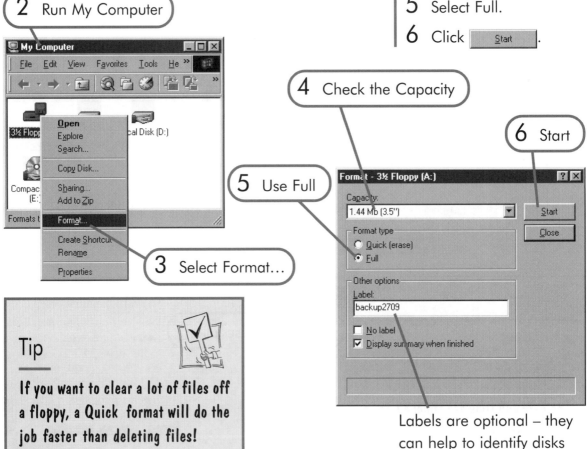

2 Run My Computer

4 Check the Capacity

6 Start

5 Use Full

3 Select Format…

Tip

If you want to clear a lot of files off a floppy, a Quick format will do the job faster than deleting files!

Labels are optional – they can help to identify disks

Caring for floppies

❏ Disk drives can be mounted horizontally or vertically, but a disk will only go in one way round. If it won't fit, don't force it. Try it the other way round.

The modern 3.5 inch floppy is quite a tough beast. Its plastic casing protects it well against grime, knocks and splashes of coffee, but it still has enemies.

● Heat, damp and magnetism will go through the casing and corrupt the data on the disk beneath. So, keep your disks away from radiators, sunny windowsills, and magnets.

● Heavy electrical machinery and mains cables should also be avoided as they too produce magnetic fields.

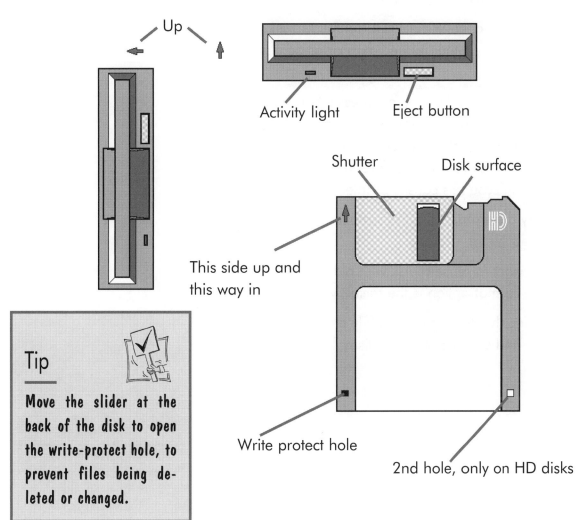

Up

Activity light   Eject button

Shutter   Disk surface

This side up and this way in

Write protect hole

2nd hole, only on HD disks

Tip

Move the slider at the back of the disk to open the write-protect hole, to prevent files being deleted or changed.

Summary

❑ Windows Me is supplied with a set of very useful system tools.

❑ Scandisk can find and fix errors on your disks.

❑ The Disk Defragmenter should be run regularly to ensure that files are stored compactly, and can therefore be loaded faster.

❑ Disk Cleanup offers an easy way to find and remove unwanted files.

❑ The Maintenance Wizard will run the housekeeping jobs for you – either immediately or as Scheduled Tasks.

❑ System Restore takes copies of essential system files so that they can be restored if necessary. This is done automatically anyway, but you can also create your own restore points before installing new software – in case this causes problems.

❑ Floppy disks must be fully formatted before they can be used.

❑ If you want to reuse a disk with old files on it, the Quick Format option is the fastest way to erase files.

❑ Floppies should be stored safely away from heat, damp and sources of magnetism.

10 Home networking

Home Networking

Setting up even a small network used to be a real chore. It got easier with the new tools introduced in Windows 95/98, but it was still not a job for the layman. It's all different with Windows Me. The Home Networking Wizard takes care of setting up the networking software and is easy to use – with two provisos.

- Networking is straightforward as long as you are connecting Windows Me PCs. You can connect to Windows 95 or 98 PCs, but you won't get quite the full range of facilities through the link. If you want to share an Internet connection, the PC with the modem must be an Me PC.

- You still have to open the PCs' cases and fit the network cards, and install their software, then cable them together.

You also need to be familiar with a few basic networking concepts. And in case you aren't, here's all you need to know...

Sharing an Internet connection

If one of the PCs has a modem and Internet connection, and you want people to be able to access this through other PCs, the connection can be shared. As long as the PC with the modem is turned on, the other networked PCs will be able to get online through it without affecting the host PC. If required, the host PC and the others can be all online at the same time through the same connection – though if several people are browsing or downloading at once, things will slow down a little.

Network names

Networked PCs must have names to identify them, which is fairly obvious. Less obvious, the whole set of linked PCs – the 'workgroup' – must also have a name. It really doesn't matter much what you call the workgroup as the name is rarely, if ever, used in a home network.

Network jargon

Workgroup – a set of linked PCs. In a home or small office, all the PCs on the network would belong to the same workgroup. The network in a larger office might be split into several workgroups.

Server – a PC providing a service to the network. A print server shares its printer; a file server acts as a storage place for the data from other PCs.

LAN (Local Area Network) – a set of PCs joined together and sharing files, printers and other facilities.

Ethernet – the most commonly used networking system.

Network hardware

❏ The simplest way to link PCs is with Ethernet cards and cable. You can buy them cheaply, and with the cable fitted with its connectors, from any good computer store. The cards go into an expansion slot – most modern PCs have PCI slots, and at least one will normally be empty.

After fitting the card, you may need to install some software that came with it – read the instructions!

The cables normally end in T-pieces, with one connection fitting to the card and the other to the next length of cable, or to a 'terminator' to end the run.

Sharing folders

You can open up some or all of the folders on a PC so that people on linked PCs can read or store files in them. In an office, open folders would be used for the files that everyone needs to be able to get at – such as the product catalogue, while those holding confidential and/or purely personal files would not be shared. In a home, you may not want to share data, but you may want to set up folders that linked PCs could use for storing backups.

In the Wizard you can either share the My Documents folder or not – with or without a password. Later you can set up sharing for any folder, and allow access at several different levels.

Sharing printers

If a printer is shared, then any networked PC can send files to it for printing. The PC to which it is attached must be turned on, of course, and the person using it may notice that it slows down a fraction as files are shuffled through the printer's folder.

Once the network is set up, use My Network Places to view the other PCs' drives – it works just like My Computer

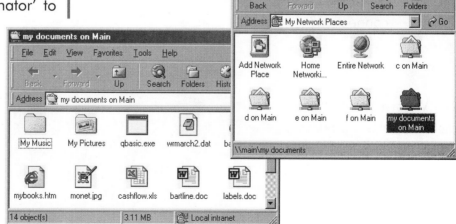

The Networking Wizard

You can set up your network over time, running the Wizard through each PC whenever you get round to it, but it is probably simpler to do it in one fell swoop. Get all the PCs going, then go round and run the Wizard on them. Watch out for these stages.

Basic steps

1 Run the Home Networking Wizard – it should be in the Accessories – Communications submenu.

2 At the Internet Connection stage, tell the Wizard if you want to use the Internet from that PC and whether it is the one with the modem.

3 On the PC with the modem, select Yes if you want other PCs to be able to use it.

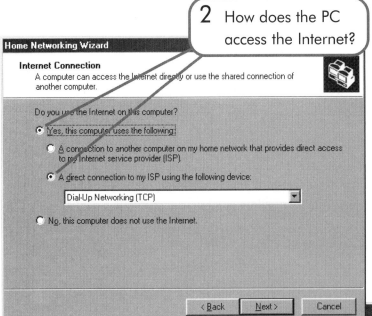

2 How does the PC access the Internet?

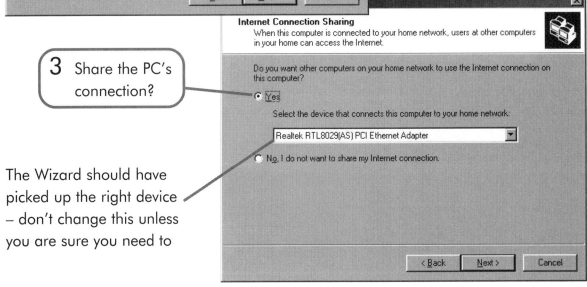

3 Share the PC's connection?

The Wizard should have picked up the right device – don't change this unless you are sure you need to

4 Give names for the computer and the workgroup.

5 Tick the checkboxes if you want to share the My Documents folder or the printer attached to the PC.

6 If you want to password protect the shared folder, click Password... and enter a password (twice).

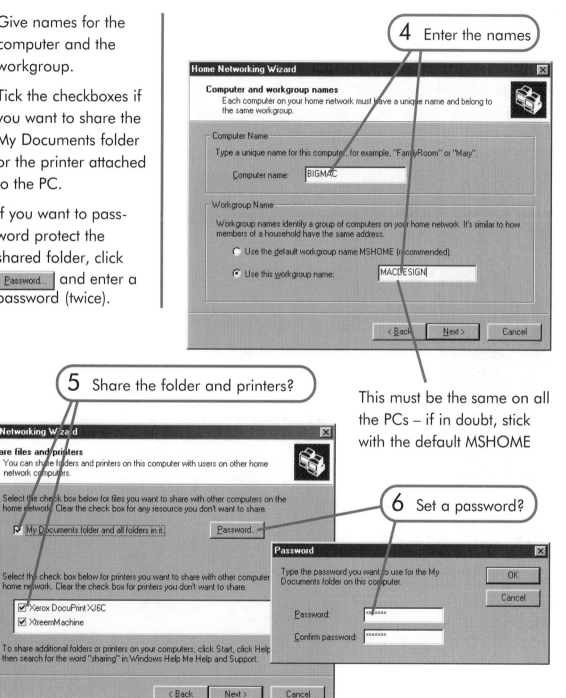

4 Enter the names

5 Share the folder and printers?

6 Set a password?

This must be the same on all the PCs – if in doubt, stick with the default MSHOME

The Internet connection

Once the network is in place, you can then run the Internet Connection Wizard on the PC that does not have the modem. Tell it you want to set up the connection manually and through a LAN (Local Area Network). When you get to the configuring stage, don't try to do it yourself – that option is there for special situations – select **Automatic discovery of proxy server** and let the Wizard sort it out for you. It may take a minute or so. The rest of the Wizard collects details of your e-mail account.

Basic steps

1 Run the Internet Connection Wizard.

2 At the first stage select *set up the connection manually.*

3 Select *connect through a LAN.*

4 Select *Automatic discovery of proxy server.*

5 If you want to use the PC for e-mail, click Yes to *set up the account* then give your account details in the following stages.

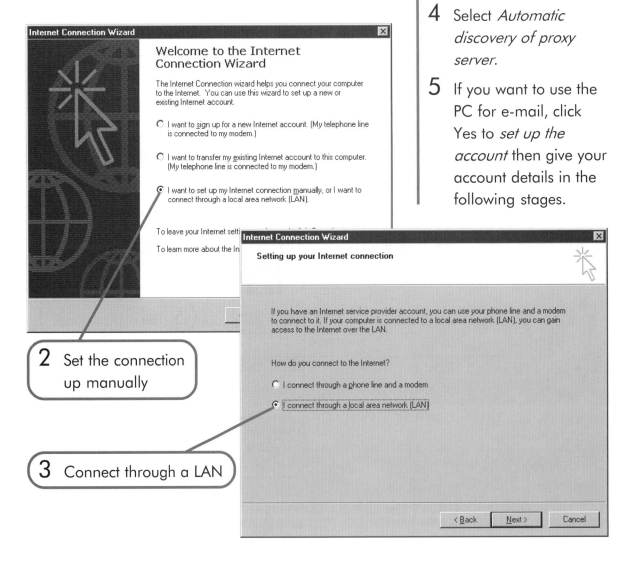

2 Set the connection up manually

3 Connect through a LAN

138

The PC with the modem is acting as a *proxy server* – it is making the connection for another PC.

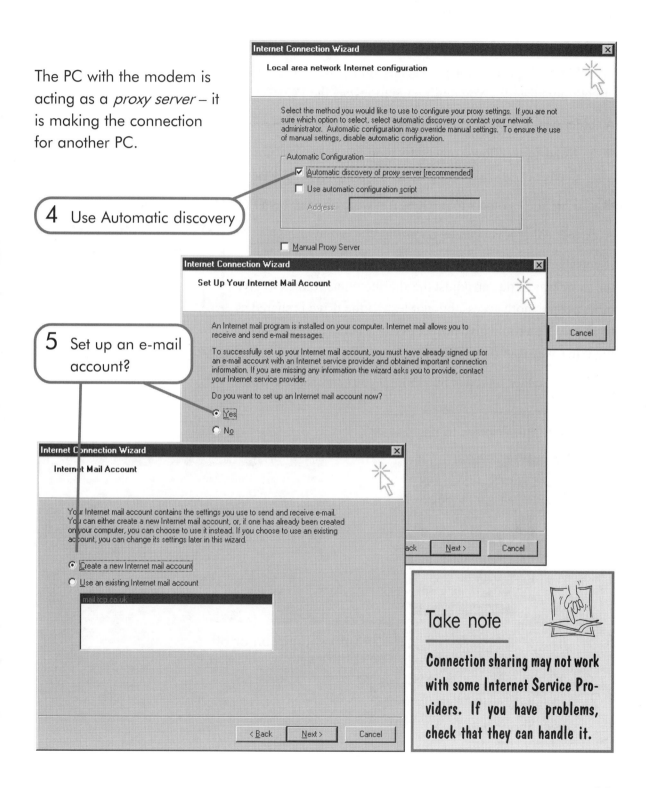

Internet Connection Wizard

Local area network Internet configuration

Select the method you would like to use to configure your proxy settings. If you are not sure which option to select, select automatic discovery or contact your network administrator. Automatic configuration may override manual settings. To ensure the use of manual settings, disable automatic configuration.

Automatic Configuration
☑ Automatic discovery of proxy server (recommended)
☐ Use automatic configuration script
Address:

4 Use Automatic discovery

☐ Manual Proxy Server

Internet Connection Wizard

Set Up Your Internet Mail Account

An Internet mail program is installed on your computer. Internet mail allows you to receive and send e-mail messages.

To successfully set up your Internet mail account, you must have already signed up for an e-mail account with an Internet service provider and obtained important connection information. If you are missing any information the wizard asks you to provide, contact your Internet service provider.

Do you want to set up an Internet mail account now?

⦿ Yes
○ No

5 Set up an e-mail account?

Cancel

Internet Connection Wizard

Internet Mail Account

Your Internet mail account contains the settings you use to send and receive e-mail. You can either create a new Internet mail account, or, if one has already been created on your computer, you can choose to use it instead. If you choose to use an existing account, you can change its settings later in this wizard.

⦿ Create a new Internet mail account
○ Use an existing Internet mail account

mail.tcp.co.uk

< Back   Next >   Cancel

Take note

Connection sharing may not work with some Internet Service Providers. If you have problems, check that they can handle it.

Sharing access

You can change the levels of access that other users can have to the folders and printers on a PC at any time. The changes take effect immediately – you don't have to restart the PC.

A folder can be shared in two ways:

● **Read-only** allows others to read its files, but not to change or delete existing files, or to save new files there.

● **Full** allows others to use it as if it were on their own PC.

Access at either level can be controlled by password.

If you share a drive, then all of its folders are initially shared in the same way. You can adjust the sharing on its folders to give other people more access, but not less. If the drive is shared as read-only, you could give full access to selected folders, but not the other way round.

Printers are either shared or not, though you can set a password.

Basic steps

❑ Sharing printers

1 Open the Printers folder from the Start – Settings menu.

2 Right-click on the printer and select Sharing...

3 Turn sharing on or off and set a password if required.

4 Click [OK].

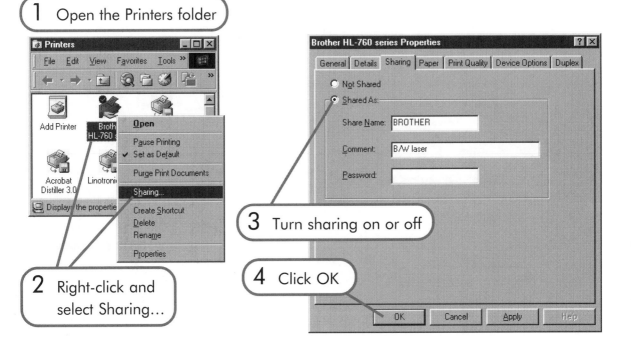

1 Open the Printers folder

2 Right-click and select Sharing...

3 Turn sharing on or off

4 Click OK

Basic steps

❑ Sharing folders

1 Run Windows Explorer or My Computer.

2 Right-click on the folder and select Sharing…

3 Set the Access Type to Read-Only, Full or Depends on Pass-word.

4 For password control-led access, set pass-words for *Read-Only* and for *Full* access – they can be the same or different, or one or other left blank.

5 Click OK.

On this PC, the whole C: drive and selected folders on D: are shared

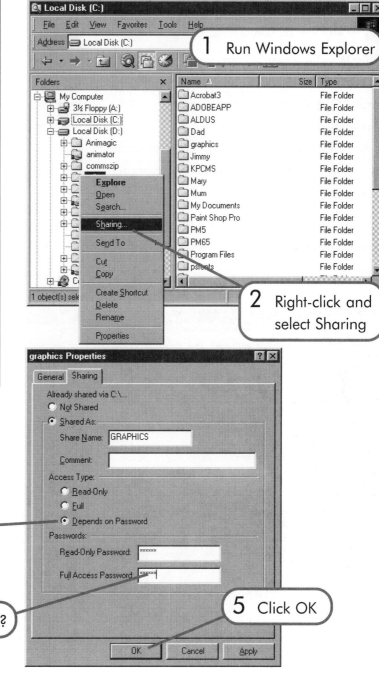

1 Run Windows Explorer

2 Right-click and select Sharing

3 Set the Access Type

4 Set Passwords?

5 Click OK

Mapped drives

Most of the newer Windows software can handle network connections with no trouble. When you want to open or save a file, these applications will let you reach across the network and link to any shared folder.

Older Windows applications were often not designed for use on networks, and will only allow you to reach files on drives on the same PC. Fortunately, Windows networking software has a neat solution to this problem. You can *map* networked drives – assign drive letters to them. The C: drive on the PC in the study, for example, which might have a network name of //Study/C/ could then be referred to as F:/ by the PC in the living room.

A drive is mapped once, from Windows Explorer, at the start of a session, and can then be referred to by its assigned letter by any application.

1 Run Windows Explorer or My Computer.

2 Right-click on the drive you want to link to and select Map Network Drive...

3 The next unused drive letter will be offered – change it only if you need to.

4 If you always need to map this drive, tick Reconnect at logon to save having to do this again.

5 Click [OK].

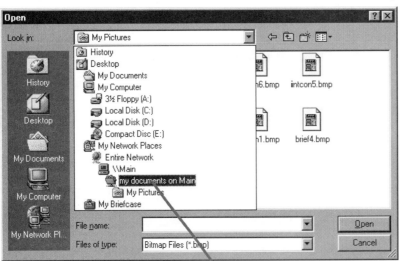

In newer applications, My Network Places is in the Look in list in Save and Open dialog boxes and you can open shared networked drives and folders directly.

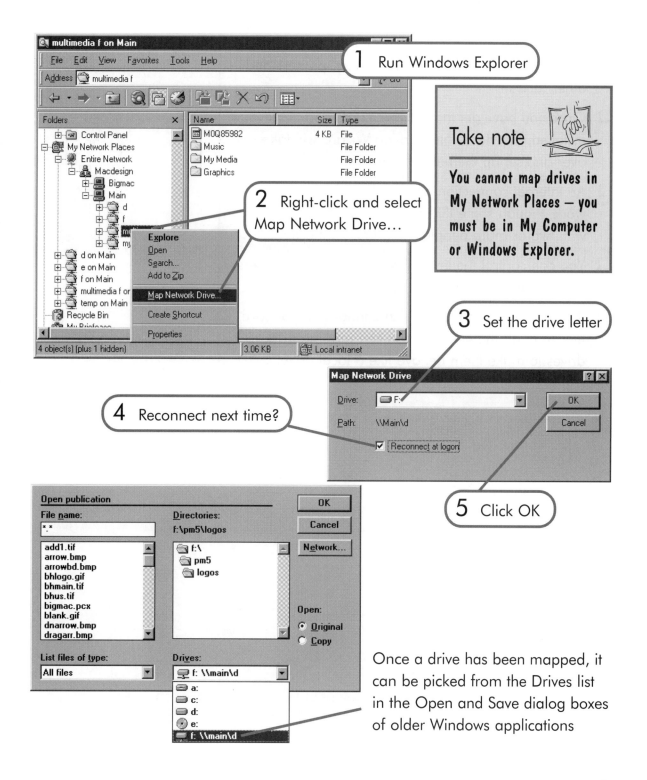

1 Run Windows Explorer

2 Right-click and select Map Network Drive...

Take note

You cannot map drives in My Network Places — you must be in My Computer or Windows Explorer.

3 Set the drive letter

4 Reconnect next time?

5 Click OK

Once a drive has been mapped, it can be picked from the Drives list in the Open and Save dialog boxes of older Windows applications

Summary

❏ Windows Me makes it simple to link PCs into a network so that you can share folders, printers and other facilities.

❏ Once you have get the network cards and cable installed, the Home Networking Wizard will take over and set up the network for you.

❏ An Internet connection can be shared over the network, though some ISPs may not be able to cope with two or more people using one connection.

❏ You can control the level of access to shared folders and printers, and change the access at any time.

❏ If you have applications which cannot open or save files through the network, you can map network drives to make them behave like a local drive.

11 The Accessories

WordPad

WordPad is a handy little word-processor, with a decent range of formatting facilities. You can set selected text in any font, size or **colour**, add emphasis with **bold**, *italics* and underline, indent paragraphs or set their alignment, and even insert pictures, clip art, charts and many other types of objects. WordPad has all you need for writing letters, essays, memos, reports and the like. Could you write a book on it? Possibly, as long as it had a simple layout and you were happy to create the contents list and index by hand.

The fact is that most of us, most of the time, use only a fraction of the facilities of Word or similar full-blown word-processors. For most purposes it is more efficient to use WordPad – because it is simpler, it is faster to load and to run – and it's faster to learn!

Tip

WordPad is a good tool for creating and editing the HTML — the coded text that produces Web pages.

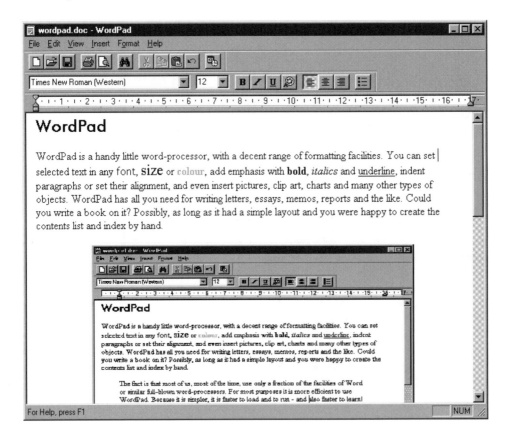

Entering text

Tip

One of the great things about Windows applications — especially those from Microsoft — is that they do the same jobs in the same way. Once you have learnt how to enter text, open or save a file, select a font or whatever, in one application, you will know how to do it in the next.

All word-processors have *wordwrap*. Don't press the [Enter] key as you get close to the right margin. WordPad will sense when a word is going to go over the end of a line and wrap it round to the start of the next. The only time you should press [Enter] is at the end of a paragragh or to create a blank line. If you change the margins of the page or the size of the font, WordPad will shuffle the text to fit, wordwrapping as it goes.

Selecting text

A block of text – anything from a single character to the whole document – is selected when it is highlighted. Once selected the text can be formatted, copied, deleted or moved.

When setting alignment or indents, which can only apply to whole paragraphs, it is enough to place the insertion point – the flashing vertical line where you type – into the paragraph.

The simplest way to select text is to drag the mouse pointer over it. Take care if some of the text is below the visible area, as the scrolling can run away with you!

A good alternative is to click the insertion point into place at the start of the block you want to select, then hold down **[Shift]** and use the arrow keys to move the highlight to the end of the block.

Double-click to select a word.

Triple-click to select a paragraph.

Deleting errors

To correct mistakes, press the **[Backspace]** key to remove the last character you typed, or select the unwanted text and press either **[Backspace]** or **[Delete]**.

Formatting text

You can do formatting in two ways – either select existing text and apply the format to it, or set up the format then start typing. Either way, the formats are selected in the same way.

Use the **Formatting toolbar** when you want to change one aspect of the formatting – just click on the appropriate button or select from the drop-down lists.

Use The **Font dialog box** when you want to define several aspects, or if you want the rarely-used strikeout effect.

Basic steps

1 Select the text or go to where the new format is to start.

2 Use the Formatting tools.

Or

3 Select Font...from the Format menu.

4 Define the format and click [OK].

2 Click or pick from a list

Underline

Font size   Italic   Colour   Alignment

Font   Bold   Left Centre Right

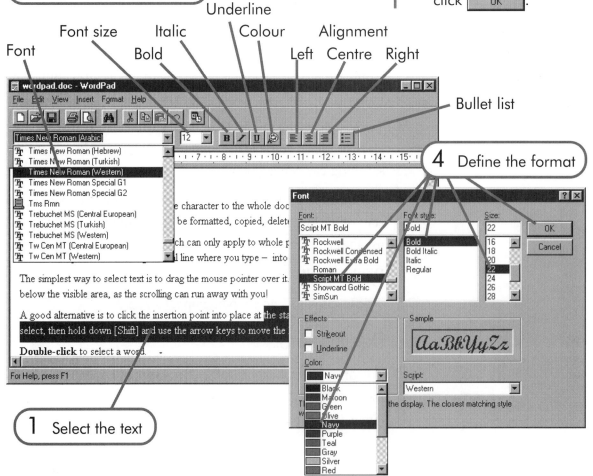

Bullet list

4 Define the format

1 Select the text

148

Basic steps

❑ Saving a new file

1 Open the File menu and select Save As...

2 Select the Save In folder.

3 Type in a Name to identify the file clearly.

4 Change the Save as type if necessary.

5 Click [Save].

❑ Resaving a file

6 Open the File menu and select Save.

Or

7 Click 🖫 the Save button on the toolbar.

File – Save and File – Save As

Anything you type into WordPad – or most other applications – is lost when you close the application unless you save the document as a file on a disk.

The first time that you save a file, you have to tell the system where to put it and what to call it. If you then edit it and want to store it on disk again, you can use a simple **File – Save** command to resave it with the same name in the same place, i.e. overwriting the old file. If you have edited a file and want to keep the old copy and the new one, then you can use **File – Save As** and save the new version under a different name.

In WordPad – again, as in many applications – you can save a file in several ways. The default is as a Word 6 document, and this should normally be used. If you want to be able to open the file in another application (not WordPad or Word), save it as plain text, Rich Text and Unicode Text. Plain text just saves the characters; the other two retain the formatting information.

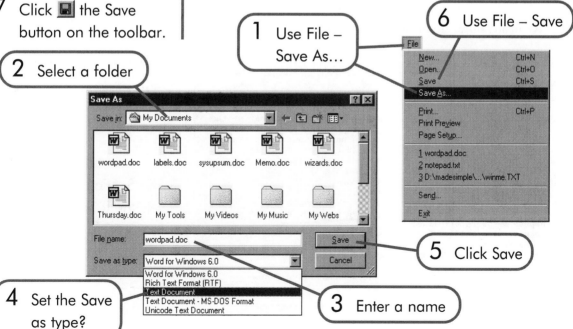

1 Use File – Save As...

6 Use File – Save

2 Select a folder

5 Click Save

4 Set the Save as type?

3 Enter a name

NotePad

Notepad is a text editor – not a word-processor – and is an excellent tool if all you want is plain text. It won't do bold or italics or fancy fonts; you can't change the size or colour of the words; it doesn't let you insert clip art or draw diagrams or set text in bullet points. Notepad gives you nothing but plain text files, and that's the beauty of it. Because it is so simple, it is a very small program – just over 50Kb – which is minute compared to Word (8Mb!). Notepad is up and running almost instantly and uses a tiny amount of your system resources.

Use Notepad instead of a word-processor:

● if you have a Hotmail (or other Web-based mail) account and want to compose messages off-line;

● to stash the text copied from Web pages, if you want to edit it before saving it;

● to write the source code for programs in Java, C or other languages;

● or in any other situation where you need unformatted text.

Take note

Notepad can only handle files up to 64Kb - but as that equates to around 9,000 words, it's not too serious a limitation.

Tip

If you want to save the whole of a Web page's text, save the page directly from Internet Explorer – just open the File menu and select Save.

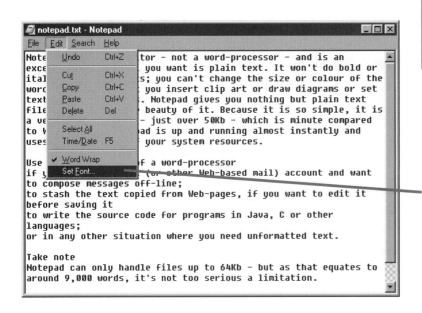

The Set Font… command sets the font used by Notepad for the screen display and printouts. The font is applied to the whole text and is not saved with the file.

Basic steps

Character Map

The Character Map

1 Go to the Accessories menu and select Character Map.

2 Select the Font.

3 Click on a character to highlight it.

4 Click [Select] to place it into Characters to Copy.

5 Go back over Steps 3 and 4 as necessary.

6 Click [Copy] to copy to the Clipboard.

7 Return to your application and Paste the characters into it.

This shows the full set of characters that are present in any given font, and allows you to select one or more individual characters for copying into other applications. Its main use is probably for picking up Wingdings for decoration, or the odd foreign letter or mathematical symbols in otherwise straight text.

The characters are rather small, but you can get a better look at a character, by holding the mouse button down while you point at it. This produces an enlarged image.

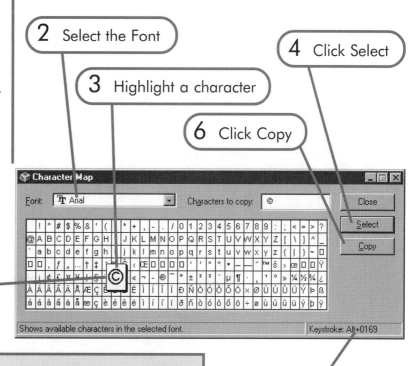

2 Select the Font

3 Highlight a character

4 Click Select

6 Click Copy

Hold down the button to magnify

Note the keystroke

Paint

There are essentially two ways to draw an image on a computer. In applications like Microsoft Draw (supplied with Works, Word and other Office programs), the picture is made up of lines, circles, text notes, etc., each of which remain separate, and can be moved, deleted, recoloured or resized at any point.

Paint uses the alternative approach. Here the image is produced by applying colour to a background, with each new line overwriting anything that may be beneath. Using this type of graphics software is very like real painting. You can wipe out a mistake while the paint is still wet, but as soon as it has dried it is fixed on the canvas. (Paint allows you to undo the last move; some will let you backtrack further.)

Tip

Press [Prt Sc] to copy the whole screen to the Clipboard, or [Alt] + [Prt Sc] to copy the active window. The image can be pasted into Paint and saved. That's how the screenshots were produced for this book.

Use the Text toolbar to format text

Ovals are defined by marking the rectangle that they will fit into, making it almost impossible to draw concentric circles. This target was created by drawing the inner circles elsewhere on the screen, then select them and dragging them into place.

Basic steps

❑ Drawing a curve

1 Draw a line between the points where the curve will start and end.

2 Click or drag to create the first curve – exaggerate the curve as it will be reduced at the next stage.

3 Drag out the second curve now – as long as the mouse button is down, the line will flex to follow the cursor.

Or

4 For a single curve, just click at the end of the line.

Tip

Hold down [Shift] when drawing for regular shapes – [Shift] makes ovals into circles; rectangles into squares and only allows lines to be drawn at 0°, 45° and 90°.

The Toolbox

There is a simple but adequate set of tools. A little experimentation will show how they all work. The curved line tool is a bit trickier than the rest. Even when you have the hang of how this works, it will still take you several goes to get a line right!

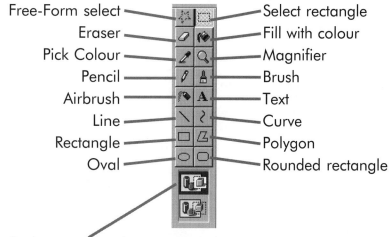

Free-Form select — Select rectangle
Eraser — Fill with colour
Pick Colour — Magnifier
Pencil — Brush
Airbrush — Text
Line — Curve
Rectangle — Polygon
Oval — Rounded rectangle

Option area used to set:
transparent or opaque background for selections;
the size of the Eraser, Brush, Airbrush and Line;
the Magnifier to 2×, 6× or 8×;
the Closed shapes to outline or fill only, or both.

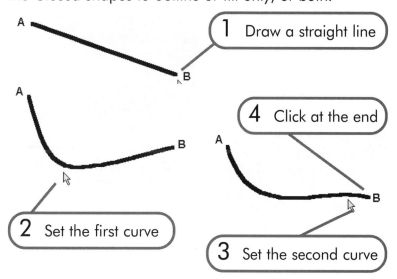

1 Draw a straight line

2 Set the first curve

4 Click at the end

3 Set the second curve

Colours

The colour palette is used in almost the same way in all Windows programs. You can select a colour from the palette – use the left button for the foreground colour and the right button for the background –or mix your own. Remember that you are mixing light, not paint.

- red and green make yellow;
- green and blue make cyan;
- blue and red make magenta;
- red, green and blue make white;
- the more you use, the lighter the colour.

❑ Mixing colours

1 Double-click on a colour in the palette or use Colors – Edit Colors.

2 At the Edit Colors dialog box, click on a Basic or Custom Color and go to step 6.

Or

3 Click `Define Custom Colors >>` to open the full box.

4 Drag the cross-hair cursor in the main square to set the Red/ Green/Blue balance, and move the arrow up or down the left scale to set the light/ dark level.

5 Click `Add to Custom Colors` if you want to add this to the set.

6 Click `OK` – the new colour will re-place the one currently selected in the palette on the main screen.

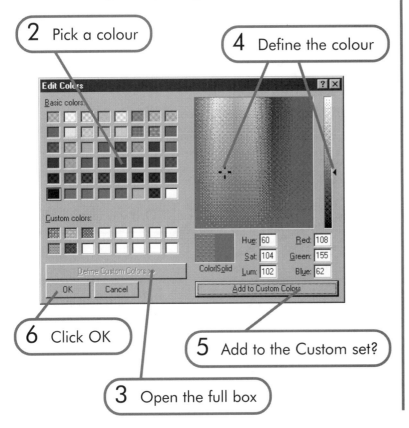

2 Pick a colour

4 Define the colour

6 Click OK

5 Add to the Custom set?

3 Open the full box

154

Media Player

Basic steps

❑ Playing CDs

1 Click the CD Audio button.

2 Load the CD and wait for Media Player to read the track data.

3 To change the order of a track, click on it, then drag up or down.

4 To skip over a track, right-click on it, and choose Disable from the shortcut menu.

Media Player is a multi-purpose audio/video player. It can handle sound files in MIDI and in WAVE, the native Windows format, as well as audio CDs and video in the Video for Windows (AVI), Media Audio/Video (WMA and ASF) or the many ActiveMovie formats.

CD audio

If you want music while you work, let Media Player play a CD for you. The CD will play the tracks in their playlist sequence – this can be the standard order or edited as required. It's worth taking time over this, as any choices or other information that you enter here are recorded by Windows in a file (stored on the hard disk) and will be reused next time the same CD is loaded.

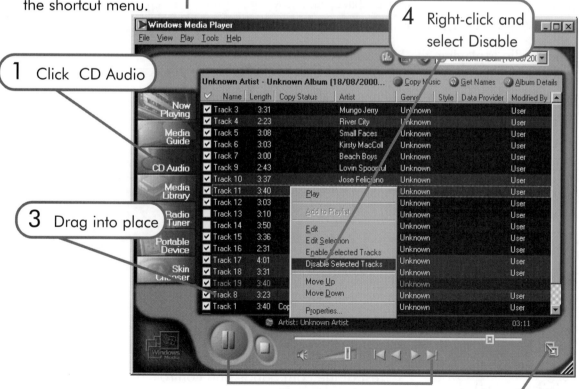

1 Click CD Audio

3 Drag into place

4 Right-click and select Disable

Play controls   Compact mode

Video

New, fast hardware and better software has greatly improved the quality of videos on PC. They are still not that brilliant to look at, but the files are relatively small. 1Mb of video gives around 90 seconds of playing time, and if you are downloading it over the Internet – from a Web site or via e-mail – it will take up to 10 minutes to come in. That's not a bad download to play time ratio. It makes it quite feasible to e-mail home movies to distant relatives – or to put them on your Web page for any friends (or visiting strangers) to downloading. And there's Movie Maker to do the editing – see opposite.

Skins

Once the video or CD is playing, you can switch into *Compact mode*. This occupies less screen space, and has some great 'skins'. Click **Skin Chooser** and pick one from the list.

When audio is playing, the Media Player screen displays a 'visualization' – a light show that responds to the music. There are dozens of these. To try them, open the View menu, point to Visualization, select a set then pick from one there. Their names are a poor guide as to their nature. You have to watch them to see what they are like.

Tip

CD audio tracks and files, from the Internet or elsewhere, in MP3, WAV, WMA or ASF formats can be copied through Media Player onto your MP3 player or other portable device.

Take note

The Radio Tuner is simply another way to get to the Internet Radio facility (see page 174).

In Compact mode, Media Player runs in a skin (above) with a minimal set of play controls. The rest of the commands and controls are reached through the icon (right)

Movie Maker

This can edit digital video, taking images in directly from your camera. The video is automatically split into clips, which can be split further or trimmed and set into a new sequence. You can merge in other clips, or add still pictures, for titles and credits, or a voice-over or background music. It's simple to use, and just the job for editing home video. Trim the half-hour birthday video down to the highlights, add your titles and voice over and save it as a Movie Maker file. You can then share it with your distant friends and relatives via the Internet in two ways:

● Send it by e-mail. Files are increased in size by 50% when attached to a message (because of the way data travels via mail), but e-mail normally comes in at 3Kb+ per second.

● Upload the file to your home page. Download times from the Web are typically less than 2Kb per second.

Movie Maker is simple to use, but efficient. It's a shame the picture quality isn't quite there yet.

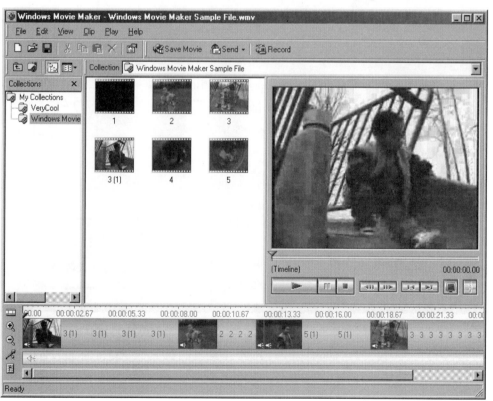

The Clipboard

The Clipboard is a mechanism for copying and moving text, graphics, files, folders and other types of data within and between applications. Whatever you are doing in Windows, it is always at hand and used in the same way.

Any Windows application that handles data in any form has an Edit menu. This always contains three core options – Cut, Copy and Paste – plus varying others. You can see these on the two Edit menus shown below.

- **Cut** removes a selected block of text or object, and transfers it to the Clipboard's memory.

- **Copy** takes a copy of the selected item into the Clipboard, but without removing it.

- **Paste** copies whatever is in the Clipboard into the current cursor position in the application.

❑ To Cut

1 Select the text or object.

2 Open the Edit menu and click Cut.

❑ To Copy

1 Select the text or object.

2 Open the Edit menu and click Copy.

❑ To Paste from the Clipboard

1 Place the cursor at the point where you want the selected item to be inserted.

2 Open the Edit menu and click Paste.

The Edit menus from Paint (left) and WordPad (below). The core options are always there.

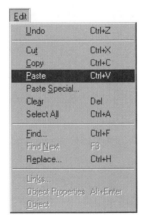

Take note

Cut and Copy are only available after you have selected something. Paste is only available if there is something in the Clipboard.

Basic steps

❏ To select text

1 Place the text cursor at the start of the block.

2 Drag the pointer to spread a highlight over the block. You are ready to Cut or Copy.

❏ To select one object

1 Click on it to get handles around its edges.

❏ To select a set of adjacent objects

1 Imagine a rectangle that will enclose all the objects.

2 Place the pointer at one corner of this rectangle.

3 Drag the broken outline to enclose them all.

4 Release the mouse button and check that all have acquired handles.

Selecting for Cut and Copy

These techniques work with most Windows applications. Some will also offer additional selection methods of their own, which may be more convenient in some situations.

You normally select **text** by dragging the pointer over the desired block of characters.

The highlight shows the selected text.

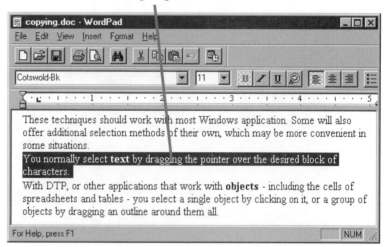

With desktop publishing, drawing software or other applications that work with **objects** – including the cells of spreadsheets and tables – you select a single object by clicking on it, or a group of objects by dragging an outline around them all.

Selected objects are usually indicated by handles.

The enclosing outline

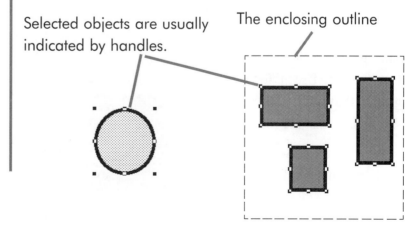

159

MS-DOS programs

Some DOS programs can be run directly from within Windows Me, simply by adding them to the Start menu. Set them to run in a Window, rather than Full Screen, to gives you access to the Edit facilities. The number of screen lines and the font can be adjusted to suit yourself.

❑ Setting up

1 Open the Properties dialog box for the program's shortcut.

2 Switch to the Screen panel.

3 Check that the Usage is set to Window.

4 Set the Initial size.

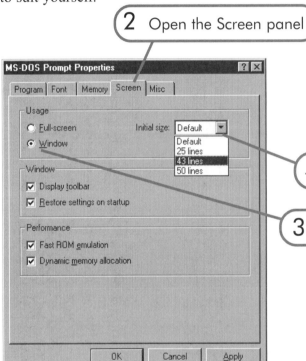

2 Open the Screen panel

4 Set the Size

3 Run in a window

Turn on the Toolbar in DOS windows for easy editing and font control.

The MS-DOS Prompt

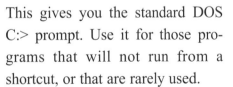

This gives you the standard DOS C:> prompt. Use it for those programs that will not run from a shortcut, or that are rarely used.

Make sure the MS-DOS Prompt is set to run in a window.

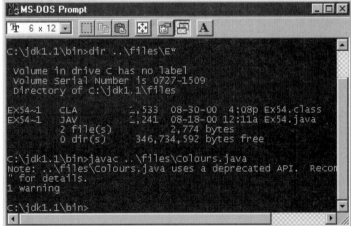

Basic steps

❑ Copying

1 Open the Control menu.

2 Select Edit, then Mark.

3 Highlight the text you want to copy.

4 Open the Control menu again and select Edit – Copy or press [Enter].

5 Switch to your target application and paste the text there.

Copy and Paste in MS-DOS

There is an Edit item in the Control menu in DOS windows, and a set of Toolbar icons that can be used to copy text between DOS and Windows applications. Pasting is the same as normal, but to copy you must first use **Edit** – **Mark** to highlight the block of text. To do this, imagine a rectangle that encloses the text. Point to one corner and drag the highlight to the opposite corner.

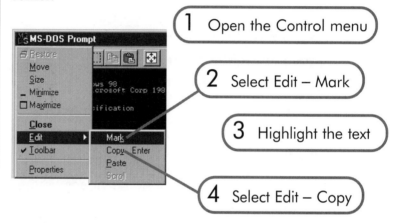

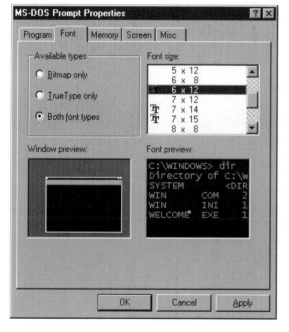

Fonts

The **A** icon on the Toolbar takes you to the Font property panel of the MS-DOS window. Note that the window's size varies with the font size, so that it holds the same quantity of text. The **Window Preview** shows the size of the window relative to the whole screen.

Summary

- ❑ WordPad is a powerful little word-processor with all the facilities that most of us need most of the time.

- ❑ Notepad is a text editor – a very efficient tool for handling plain text files.

- ❑ The Character map allows you to select special characters from a selected font, to paste into an application.

- ❑ You can use Paint for creating simple (or complex if you're good enough!) colourful pictures or for editing screenshots and other images.

- ❑ Media Player will play audio CDs, radio braodcasts or videos. The player can be run in compact mode, in a colourful skin.

- ❑ With Movie Maker you can edit home videos before sending them to friends via the Internet.

- ❑ The Clipboard is used for copying text and graphics within and between programs, and for copying files and folders across disks and folders.

- ❑ Text can be selected by dragging a highlight over it.

- ❑ Individual images and files can be selected by clicking on them. Groups of objects can be selected by dragging outlines around them.

- ❑ MS-DOS programs can be run directly from shortcuts, or through the MS-DOS prompt. In either case, they should be set to run in a window, not full screen, to get access to the cut and paste facilities.

12 Exploring the Internet

Take note

To get online, you must have an account with an Internet Service Provider. If you do not have one already, you will find all you need to connect to AOL in the Online Services folder, and a link to MSN on the Desktop. AOL offers a free month's trial — give it a go.

Internet Explorer (IE)

Internet Explorer is a browser – software for viewing pages on the World Wide Web. IE5.5 (the current version) is very easy to use.

The main part of the window is used for the display of Web pages. Above this are the control elements. The **Menu bar** contains the full command set, with the most commonly used ones duplicated in the **Standard Toolbar**.

● The **Address** shows you where you are. You can type a URL (Uniform Resource Locator – an Internet address) here to open a page. Typed URLs are stored here, for ease of revisiting.

● The **Links** offer an easy way to connect to selected places. Initially, they connect to pages on Microsoft's site, but you can replace them or add your own.

The **Toolbars** can be turned on or off as needed, but if you want the maximum viewing area click the Fullscreen icon.

The **Explorer Bar** can be opened on the left of the screen to give simpler navigation when searching the Internet (page 170), or when using the Favorites (page 168) or History (page 167).

The **Status Bar** at the bottom of the page shows how much of an incoming file has been loaded. This can also be turned off if you don't want it.

The Standard Toolbar

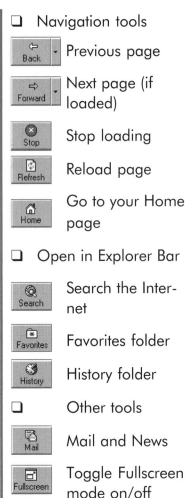

❑ Navigation tools

Previous page

Next page (if loaded)

Stop loading

Reload page

Go to your Home page

❑ Open in Explorer Bar

Search the Internet

Favorites folder

History folder

❑ Other tools

Mail and News

Toggle Fullscreen mode on/off

Print the page

Basic steps

- ❑ Display options
- **1** Click on View.
- **2** Point to Toolbar and turn them on (✓) or off from the submenu.
- **3** Click on Status Bar to turn it on or off.

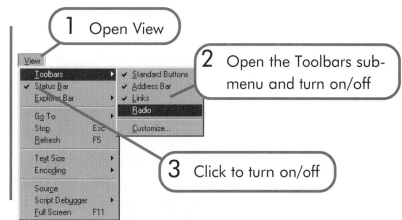

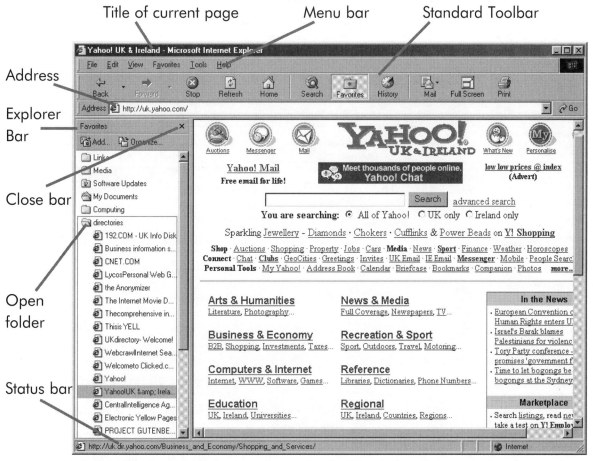

Yahoo! directories are great places for finding links. There are local ones for many countries, plus the central one at www.yahoo.com

165

Starting to explore

The World Wide Web is held together by hypertext links. These take you from one page to another – which may be within the same site or on the other side of the world.

Links are easy to recognise – the mouse pointer turns into a hand 🖑 when over a link; and even easier to use – just click on them.

But first you need a place to start! IE has some ready-made links to good starting places in the Links toolbar and the Favorites list, and if you know an address, you can type it in directly.

Basic steps

1   Run IE 🅔 from the Desktop, the Quick Launch Toolbar or the Programs menu.

2   Click on a Link.

or

3   Follow a Favorite.

or

4   Type in an Address.

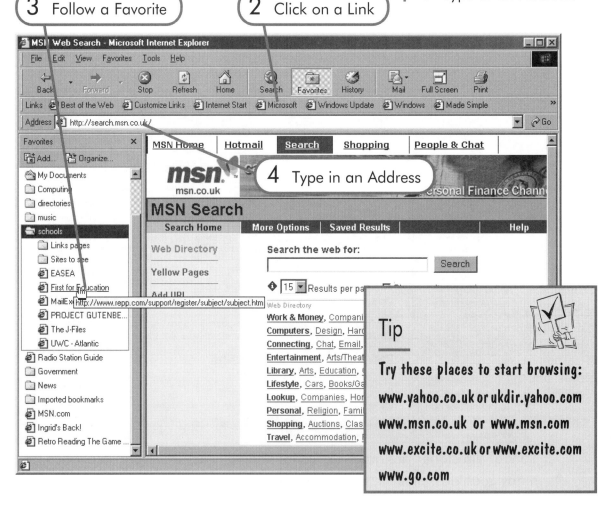

Basic steps

1 Click the History button to open the list in the Explorer Bar.

2 Click to open a site's folder.

3 Select the page.

4 Click the X at the top right of the Explorer Bar to close it.

As you browse, each page is recorded in the History list as an Internet Shortcut – i.e. a link to the page. Clicking the History button opens the list in the Explorer Bar, where the links are organised into folders, according to site.

History Offline

If you want to use the History after you have gone offline, open the File menu and turn on the Work Offline. If a page actively draws from its home site – typically to get fresh adverts – you will not be able to open it offline.

Unwanted items can be removed – right-click for the short menu and select Delete

1 Click History

2 Open a site folder

3 Pick a page

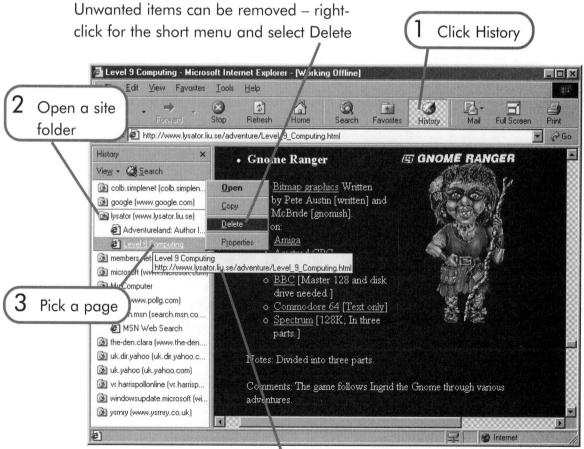

Hold the mouse over a link to see its full address

Favorites

With millions of Web pages available, finding really good ones can take time. When you do find one, you should add it to the Favorites list – this stores the address of the page so that you can get back to it quickly in future. IE has a few Favorites set up for you, to start you off.

You can access Favorites from the Menu bar, but the best way to use them is to open the Favorites list in the Explorer Bar.

● If you want to go back to a page in a later session, you can simply pick it from the Favorites menu.

● You must have the page open to be able to add it to the Favorites – but you can do this offline by opening the page from the History list.

● The Favorites are stored in a folder. If you have a lot of entries, you can organise them into new folders within this, creating submenus of Favorites.

❑ Using Favorites

1 Open Favorites and select the page title.

❑ Adding Favorites

2 Open the Favorites menu and select Add to Favorites...

Or

3 Open Favorites in the Explorer Bar and click 🖼️ Add... .

4 Edit the name.

5 To add it to the main menu, click OK .

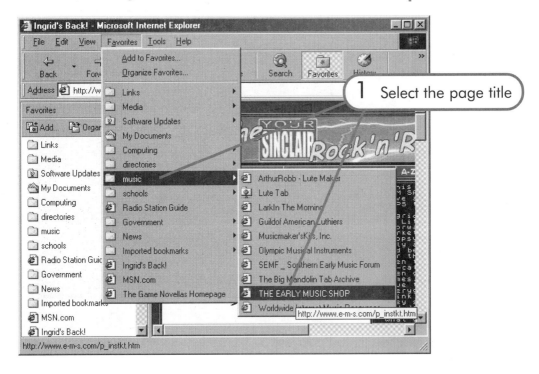

1 Select the page title

Or

6 To store it in a folder, click [Create in >>].

7 Select the folder.

8 Click [OK].

If the Favorites list gets messy, use Organize Favorites to sort it out

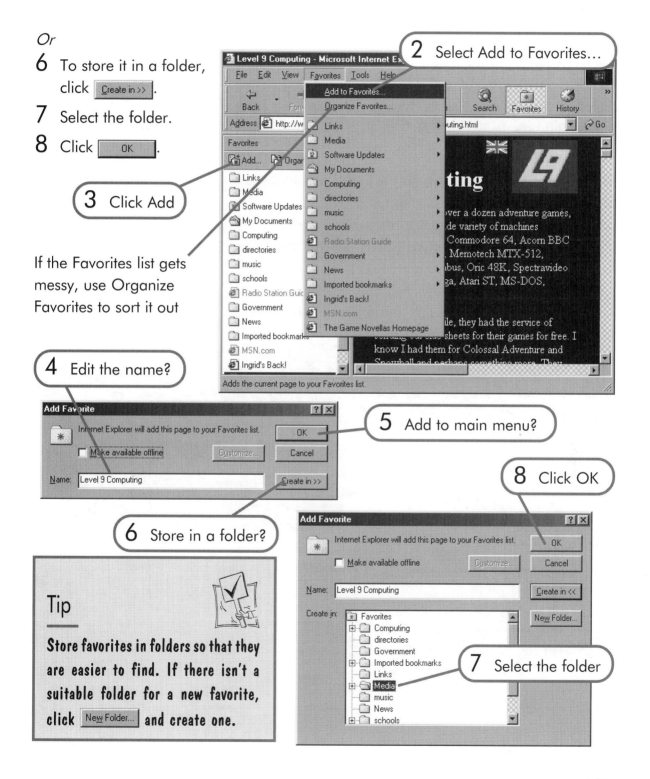

2 Select Add to Favorites...

3 Click Add

4 Edit the name?

5 Add to main menu?

8 Click OK

6 Store in a folder?

7 Select the folder

Tip

Store favorites in folders so that they are easier to find. If there isn't a suitable folder for a new favorite, click [New Folder...] and create one.

Searching in Explorer

Directories like MSN and Yahoo are good for dipping in to see what's around, but if you want specific information on a topic, you are probably better off with a search. You can run a simple search in the Explorer Bar for Web pages, maps and other things. This uses the Excite 'search engine', one of the best of many such on the Web.

The Explorer Bar is a convenient way to handle searches as you can switch easily between viewing results and running new searches, but it may not always work that well. If it doesn't find any good links – in fact, it is more likely to find too many than too few – then try working directly at a search engine, where you will be able to define your search more closely. Two of the best search sites are **www.google.com** and **www.altavista.com**.

1 Click the Search tool.

2 Select the Category.

3 Enter a keyword or phrase.

4 Click Search .

5 You are taken to Excite for the results – click a link to view the page.

6 If you don't find what you want, try a new word or widen the search to the whole Web.

It doesn't matter where you are when you start the search

1 Click Search

2 Select a Category

3 Enter the keyword(s)

4 Click Search

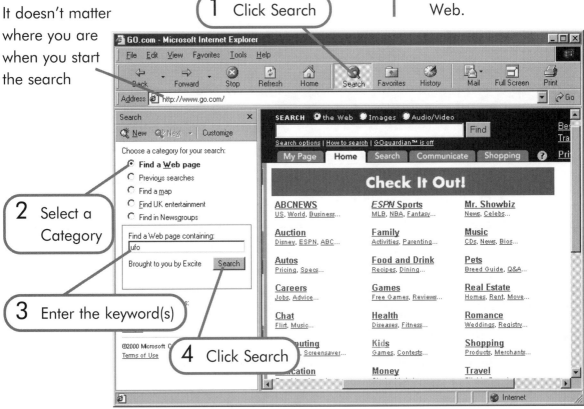

170

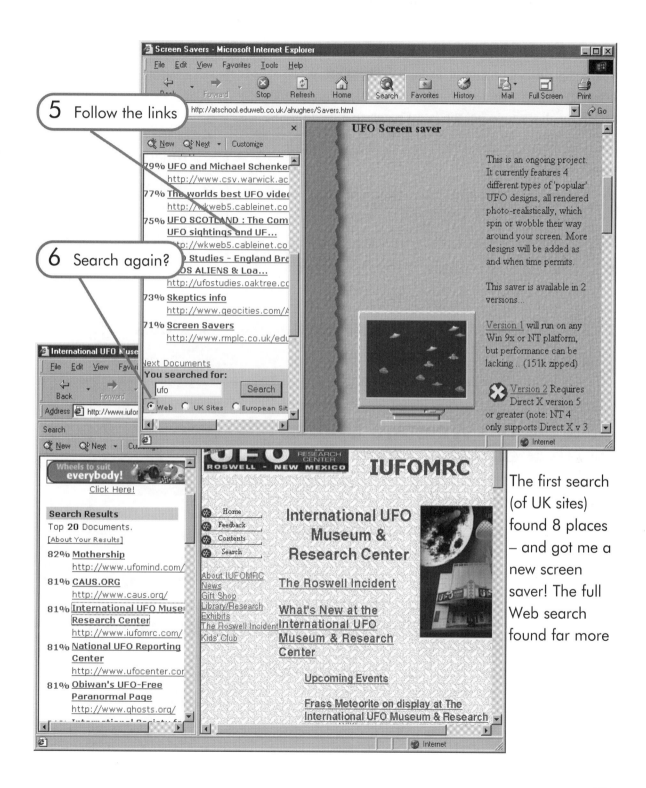

5 Follow the links

6 Search again?

171

Windows Update

Microsoft regularly produce improvements and bug-fixes for Windows, distributing them through the Internet. Windows Me has an Automatic Updates routine which can connect regularly to Microsoft's site to get the latest patches and additions.

The Automatic Updates settings can be changed through the Control Panel. It can:

Automatic Updates

- download automatically, notifying you when the files are ready to be installed;

- alert you if it finds any new critical or optional updates;

- be turned off completely, if you prefer to use the Windows Update link to check the site when it suits you.

1 Leave it to Automatic Updates to alert you.

Or

2 From **Start** select Windows Update .

3 Wait while the Update Wizard scans your PC.

4 Scroll through, ticking the updates you want and click Download.

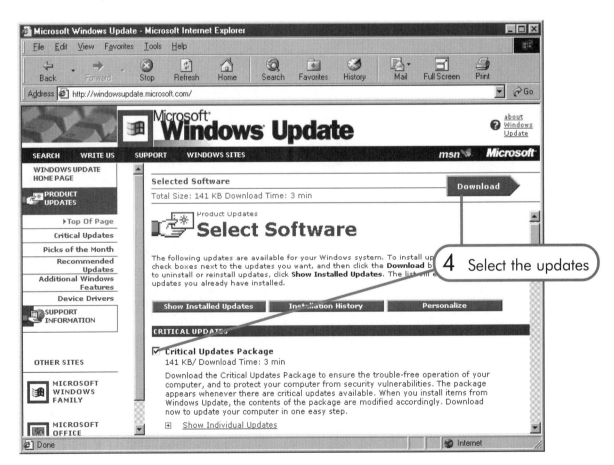

5 Check the selections in the checklist and click Start Download.

The time estimates are fairly accurate – make sure that you have enough time to get the files before you start.

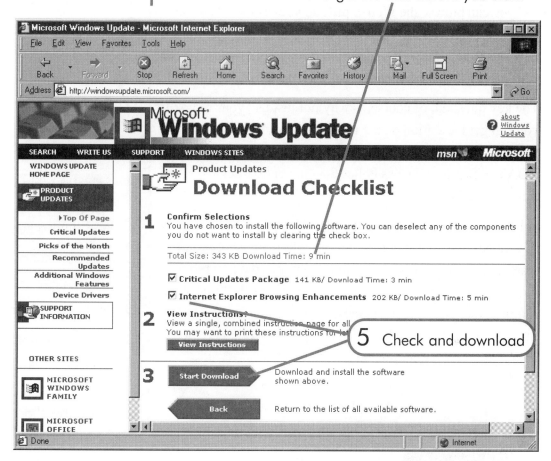

The files are downloaded and then installed automatically. You will normally have to restart the PC to bring them into play, but it doesn't have to be done immediately – finish your session as usual. At the next start up, there will probably be a delay while your system files are updated.

Radio stations

Over the last few years, new techniques have been developed for transmitting audio (and video) over the Internet in real time. Now you can listen to a 'broadcast' through Internet Explorer, and you can browse the Web or pick up your e-mail at the same time.The sound quality is as good as you would get from a portable radio, though if you are also trying to download other stuff you will get occasional breaks in transmission.

The key question, of course, is why not just use your radio? If you can get the station on the radio, it makes little sense to use your browser, but can you pick up American Family Radio, KBAY of San José, Dallas Police Scanner or OzRock? You can through the Web.

When you link to a radio station, its Web page will normally download first, with the broadcast following shortly afterwards. There will always be an initial delay as the first block of data loads in – you will see 'Buffering' in the Radio toolbar. Internet Radio is not quite in real time. Incoming data is stashed in a buffer – temporary storage – and played from there, to try to smooth out irregularities in the flow of data.

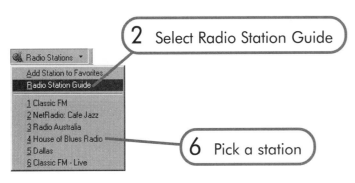

2 Select Radio Station Guide

6 Pick a station

1 Display the Radio toolbar.

❑ Finding stations

2 Click Radio Stations and select Radio Station Guide.

3 Click one of the stations in the Presets list.

Or

4 Select a <Find By> category from the list and then a sub-group.

5 Select a station and click Play > .

❑ Normal listening

6 Click Radio Stations and select a visited station from the list.

7 Drag the slider to set the volume.

8 When you have finished, or if you need to speed up other downloading, click Stop .

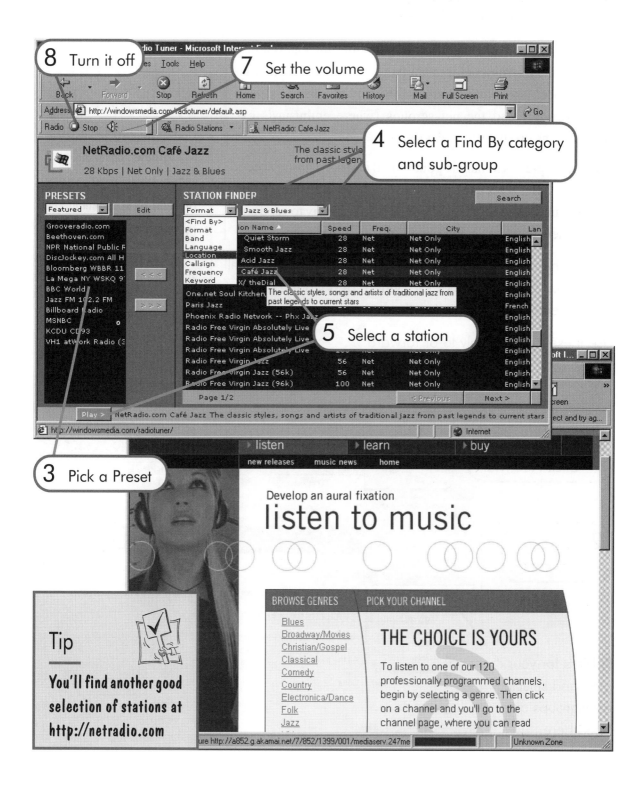

8 Turn it off

7 Set the volume

Radio Tuner - Microsoft Internet...

File Edit View Favorites Tools Help

Back | Forward | Stop | Refresh | Home | Search | Favorites | History | Mail | Full Screen | Print

Address http://windowsmedia.com/radiotuner/default.asp

Radio ◉ Stop ◀× | Radio Stations ▾ | NetRadio: Café Jazz

NetRadio.com Café Jazz

The classic style from past legen

28 Kbps | Net Only | Jazz & Blues

4 Select a Find By category and sub-group

PRESETS

Featured ▾ | Edit

Grooveradio.com
Beethoven.com
NPR National Public R
DiscJockey.com All H
Bloomberg WBBR 11
La Mega NY WSKQ 9
BBC World
Jazz FM 102.2 FM
Billboard Radio
MSNBC
KCDU CD 93
VH1 atWork Radio (3

STATION FINDER | Search

Format ▾ | Jazz & Blues ▾

<Find By>
Format
Band
Language
Location
Callsign
Frequency
Keyword

ion Name ▲	Speed	Freq.	City	Lan
Quiet Storm	28	Net	Net Only	English
Smooth Jazz	28	Net	Net Only	English
Acid Jazz	28	Net	Net Only	English
Café Jazz	28	Net	Net Only	English
X/ theDial	28	Net	Net Only	English

One.net Soul Kitchen | The classic styles, songs and artists of traditional jazz from past legends to current stars | English
Paris Jazz | | | | French
Phoenix Radio Network -- Phx Jazz | | | | English
Radio Free Virgin Absolutely Live | | | | English
Radio Free Virgin Absolutely Live | | | | English
Radio Free Virgin Absolutely Live | | | | English
Radio Free Virgin Jazz | 56 | Net | Net Only | English
Radio Free Virgin Jazz (56k) | 56 | Net | Net Only | English
Radio Free Virgin Jazz (96k) | 100 | Net | Net Only | English

5 Select a station

Page 1/2 | ‹ Previous | Next ›

Play > | NetRadio.com Café Jazz The classic styles, songs and artists of traditional jazz from past legends to current stars

http://windowsmedia.com/radiotuner/ | Internet

▸ listen | ▸ learn | ▸ buy

new releases | music news | home

3 Pick a Preset

Develop an aural fixation
listen to music

BROWSE GENRES | PICK YOUR CHANNEL

Blues
Broadway/Movies
Christian/Gospel
Classical
Comedy
Country
Electronica/Dance
Folk
Jazz

THE CHOICE IS YOURS

To listen to one of our 120
professionally programmed channels,
begin by selecting a genre. Then click
on a channel and you'll go to the
channel page, where you can read

ure http://a852.g.akamai.net/7/852/1399/001/mediaserv.247me | Unknown Zone

Tip

You'll find another good selection of stations at http://netradio.com

175

Outlook Express

The World Wide Web may be the most visible and entertaining aspect of the Internet, but it is not the only one. The other two major aspects are e-mail – which for many people is its most valuable use – and the newsgroups (where enthusiasts exchange ideas on specific topics).

Outlook Express will handle your e-mail and newsgroup access efficiently. Messages can be composed and read offline, so that you only need to connect briefly once or twice a day to send and receive new ones – keeping phone bills to a minimum.

Take note

There are over 25,000 newsgroups, covering just about every topic under the sun! Check them out — there's sure to be at least one for your job, hobby and obsession.

The headers of messages are shown here. They tell you who sent the article, when, and what it's about. Select one to read it in the lower pane.

Use these tools to reply to or forward on the current message

1 Click New Mail

2 Pick your stationery

Folders for your mail and selected newsgroups are listed here.

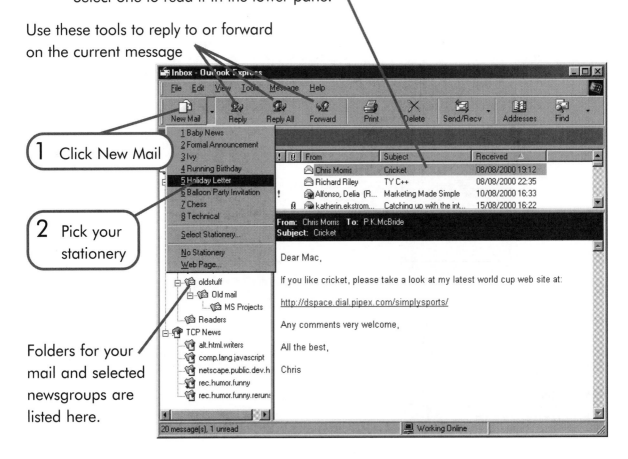

Basic steps

1 Click New Mail to send a text message.

Or

2 Select your stationery from the New Mail list.

3 Type the address or click 🔳 To: and pick it from the Address Book.

4 Type a Subject so that your recipients know what it's about when they see the header.

5 Type your message.

6 If you want to attach a file (that video?) click 🔘 and select the file.

7 Click 🔄. The message will either be sent immediately or go into the Outbox to be sent when you are next online and click 🔄▾.

Take note

Stationery can add a lot to the transfer time.

Sending a message

To send a message all you need is the address – and something to say. Actually, if you are replying to a message, you don't even need the address as Outlook will pick that off the incoming mail. Addresses can be typed in or picked out of the Address Book – click **Addresses** in the main toolbar to open it.

Messages can be composed and sent immediately if you are online, or composed offline and sent later.

Messages are normally written as plain text, but if you are writing to someone who can read HTML-formatted messages (such as another Outlook user) you can liven them up by using stationery – with backgrounds and fancy fonts.

A message can be sent to several people at once. You can put them all in the To: box, or send some as copies in the Cc: box.

3 Give the addresses

7 Click send

6 Attach a file?

4 Type a Subject

5 Type the message

Summary

❑ Internet Explorer is a Web browser. It is integrated into My Computer and Windows Explorer, so you can also start to browse from there.

❑ Browsing is simple – just follow the links – but you need a place to start. IE comes supplied with links to some good start points on the Web.

❑ The History list gives you an easy way to revisit sites – online or offline.

❑ The Favorites folder stores links to selected places on the Internet. There are some already set up and you can add your own links.

❑ You can search for stuff in the Explorer Bar, then view the resulting pages in the main screen.

❑ Go online to the Windows Update site from time to time to see if Microsoft has any new or improved versions of its Windows Me software.

❑ Many radio stations broadcast through the Web. You can listen to them in IE using the Radio toolbar.

❑ Outlook Express is the supplied software for handling e-mail and newsgroup articles.

Tip

There's lots more about Internet Explorer and Outlook Express in *Explorer 5 Made Simple*, and if you want to know more about the Internet, try *The Internet Made Simple*.

Index